PENGUIN BOOKS

THIS IS IKIGAI365

The diverse team, including Prof. Akihiro Hasegawa—Professor of clinical psychology at Teikyo University, Japan, who holds a PhD in Ikigai and has dedicated over twenty years of his life to researching it; Rajiv Bajaj—Chairman of Bajaj Capital, one of India's most trusted Financial Planning brands, a TEDx speaker, and an established Ikigai Coach; Shivendu Nadkarni—Adjunct Associate Professor at NUS Business School in Singapore, and mentor to several entrepreneurs; Sumathy Gajapathy—team's lead researcher and storyteller, an Indian-born in Chennai, who has spent over half her life in Japan, brings insights from the Japanese culture; and Rati Arora—an internationally certified health and self-care coach, and a young mother embracing the Ikigai approach to parenting—shares a common mission.

The authenticity of Ikigai365 team is deeply rooted in Prof. Hasegawa's more than two decades of extensive research on Ikigai.

While each team member has individual motivations as practitioners of Ikigai for contributing to this book, a shared passion for disseminating authentic knowledge of Japanese Ikigai is what unites them.

ADVANCE PRAISE FOR *THIS IS IKIGAI365*

'This book is a wonderful exposition of the fact that Ikigai is a celebration of each person's unique personality. It is inspiring to hear so many different voices, until we are immersed in the deeply resonant music of the orchestra that is life.'

—Ken Mogi
Author, *The Little Book of Ikigai*

'This book reinforces the same message my lengthy research does: In the second phase of life, we must *not* start to wind down in retirement; rather, we must "rewire". By "rewiring", we reawaken our purpose, and we explore new ways of feeling alive and useful, no matter our age or circumstance.

This book shares real-life stories of individuals in Japan who are quietly and powerfully living their Ikigai, through thoughtful introspection, emotional renewal and the pursuit of a life lived with meaning.

I encourage you to read it, absorb its message, and enjoy it!'

—Dr. Riley Moynes
Author, *The Four Phases of Retirement*

'Our research has shown that strong social networks are just as vital to longevity as diet or exercise. This book beautifully captures how human connection and a sense of purpose—Ikigai—can nourish us across a lifetime.'

—Dr. Makoto Suzuki
Co-author, *The Okinawa Program* and *The Okinawa Diet Plan*

'Through the wisdom of the twenty-three individuals in this book, you will find your reasons to wake up each morning. If you want to have a meaningful life, read this book.'

—Eric Sim
Author, *Small Actions*

'A graceful, grounded guide to living with meaning. *This Is Ikigai365* weaves timeless insight with heartfelt stories—quietly powerful, deeply personal, and beautifully practical.'

—Dandapani
Author, *The Power of Unwavering Focus*

'I have known Rajiv for several years and he is a genuine practitioner and explorer of Ikigai and has instilled these principles in his own life as well as lives of thousands of others.

This book is a true result of the years of deep research that he has done in the subject and has the potential of transforming every life.

I recommend this book to everyone.'

—Ira Trivedi
Best-selling author, Yoga acharya

'The people in this book are just living their everyday lives. But their stories, the ways they live, are inspirational! From now on, I want to learn to love every moment of my life.'

—Yew Chong Yip
Mural artist

THIS IS IKIGAI365

Your Journey to Feeling Alive and Fulfilled Everyday

Prof. Akihiro Hasegawa, Rajiv Bajaj,
Rati Arora, Shivendu Nadkarni,
Sumathy Gajapathy

PENGUIN BOOKS

An imprint of Penguin Random House

PENGUIN BOOKS

Penguin Books is an imprint of the Penguin Random House group of companies whose
addresses can be found at global.penguinrandomhouse.com

Published by Penguin Random House SEA Pte Ltd
40 Penjuru Lane, #03-12, Block 2
Singapore 609216

First published in Penguin Books by Penguin Random House SEA 2025

ISBN 9789815323061

Typeset in Adobe Garamond Pro by MAP Systems, Bengaluru, India

www.penguin.sg

Opening Note

Are you ready to experience something unexpected? A combination of learning with logic and feeling the magic of Ikigai journeys awaits you.

Imagine your mood suddenly lifted by a song, when you least expect it. The song 'Ikigai' by Chiharu Matsuyama has an enchanting theme which, from the interplay between life and seasons, you will feel an instant connection with.

The same has inspired the structure of the book.

We hope your Ikigai exploration journey through the stories and the journal is also filled with the magic of dreams, nature, and whatever inspiration you discover in the process that makes you feel alive—no matter what your season of life you are in.

Contents

Opening Note   vii
Foreword   xiii
Introduction   xv
History of Ikigai   xxi
Kamiya Mieko, The Mother of Modern Ikigai   xxv
Three Elements of Ikigai Model and Ikigai365 Framework   xxvii

Part 1: Stories

Chapter 1 – Spring   3
   Life Worth ≠ Net Worth   5
   Connections that Celebrate Generations   19
   Feeling Alive Here-And-Now = Life Without Regrets   27
   Short Story: True Caring = Guilt-Free Self-Care   37
   Short Story: Building Happier Workplaces   39

Chapter 2 – Summer   45
   Caring is the Ultimate Form of Giving   47
   Smile of Gratitude Lights up the Heart   57
   'Creating My Own *Ibasho* - A Place to Belong'   67
   Short Story: Balance Impact With Connection   77
   Short Story: Strength + Beauty = Self-Worth   81

Chapter 3 – Autumn   85

Life Becomes Worthy When You Start 'Living It'   87

Rewire – Don't Retire   95

'Somehow . . . It All Works Out'   103

My Life. My Pace. My Stage. My Sanctuary   111

Short Story: Fragility of Life Fuels Spirit of Innovation   121

Short Story: Kimono-Inspired Vitality   123

Short Story: Learning ∞ Sharing Cycle
Drives Youthfulness   127

Chapter 4 – Winter   129

Curiosity is Ageless   133

Giving Feels Like Receiving   141

Making Life an 'Eternal Spring'   149

Craft A Beautiful Life . . . One Day at a Time   159

Short Story: Preserving Memories, Not Counting Years   165

Short Story: Authenticity Breeds Resilience in Service   169

Epilogue   175

Why We Wrote This Book   181

Why We Wrote This Book Together As a Team   191

Part 2: myIkigai365 Nourishment Journal
Ikigai365 Moments Toolkit (10-15 minutes)

What Makes Your Heart Smile   200

Coffee Date with Yourself   202

Ikigai365 Tune-in Toolkit (20-30 minutes)

Design Your Beautiful Day 203

Iki-ga-ii-na: Savour the Moment with Six Senses 205

**Ikigai365 myPace Nourishment Toolkit
(60 minutes or longer)**

Letter from Your Future Self 209

Doh-Sa Therapy Practice 215

Connecting The Dots 221

Lifeline Mapping 227

Ikigai > Hatarakigai 229

Fill Your Cup (with more and more Ikigai sources) 231

Ikigai365 Reflections > Action Tool 232

Endnotes 235

Foreword

By His Holiness Dalai Lama

I am happy to see a book on Ikigai written by Team Ikigai365, comprising Japanese and Indian practitioners, who wish to spread the message of positive living by informing people about this time-honoured Japanese way of living a life of purpose, meaning, and joy. It is heartening to learn that Ikigai accords with scientific finding as well.

It is my conviction that warm-hearted concern for others' well-being is the key not only to our own happiness, but also to our survival. Real change in the world only comes from a change of heart. That means thoughts and actions motivated by altruistic intentions are indispensable for fulfilling our goals in life.

Honesty, kindness, and ethical conduct are essential for a good life. Through love and compassion, you will have sown a deep seed that will cause you to care about the suffering of others. Understanding the interdependent nature of life allows you to put others before yourself and to put aside all selfish motive, while embracing altruism and concern for others' well-being.

One of the core principles in Buddhism is to bring benefit to others—or if that is not possible, at least to do no harm—while kindness, compassion and integrity are the very heart of its practice.

I understand that Ikigai is about finding a meaningful life with warm heartedness. We are interconnected social animals, and therefore, serving and helping others is a skilful way of attaining our own happiness and peace of mind.

In my opinion, the purpose and meaning of our life is to be happy, and that true happiness results from a peace of mind underpinned by a compassionate heart. This is most important for a fulfilled life. A truly meaningful life is ensured by our concern for the well-being of all sentient beings, especially the poor and the needy.

I hope readers of this book will find it helpful in bringing about a better and altruistic way of life.

16 June 2025

Introduction

Thank you for picking up this book.

It is great to have you here, and we are excited to be able to share with you an authentic exploration of the Japanese perspective on Ikigai. We hope you will get a glimpse into the everyday life experiences of normal people—like you and us—and get a feel for how people in Japan create their own unique Ikigai journeys.

Before we dive in, a quick glance at the etymology of the term Ikigai. It's a complex word that means different things to different people, based on their own life journeys and perspectives.

But how would you interpret Ikigai, based on the kanjis below?

The Japanese dictionary, *daijirin,* defines Ikigai as 'life worth living'.

'Iki' (生き: life, living, birth, genuine) with the addition of 'kai' (かい: worth, value).

An interdisciplinary concept that blends psychology, psychiatry, and philosophy, while Ikigai's roots are in Japan, the concept is universal. It is humanely evergreen in nature, a deeply personal and individual concept that revolves around understanding what gives our lives meaning and purpose. Because it touches on both psychology and one's beliefs, Ikigai is unique to each individual, and therefore, shaped by their thoughts, feelings, and life experiences. Its beauty lies in its authenticity that guides this personal journey towards making every day worth living.

Prof. Akihiro Hasegawa, one of the authors of this book, has spent over twenty years undertaking modern-day research on Ikigai. His ideas and expertise are the backbone of Ikigai365 and have helped lead to the stories and tools you will experience in this book. The practical anchor of Hasegawa-*san*'s Ikigai work is the continuum of PAST–PRESENT–FUTURE.

For example, a widow who lost her husband after decades of marriage might find a source of Ikigai by reliving the memories of their annual holiday trips. This could involve looking through old photographs from the PAST, as well as revisiting the same places they once travelled together.

Or for someone who is at the peak of their career, their PRESENT job and the challenges and rewards it brings may be the source of their Ikigai.

Or for a mother with a school-going child, aspirations and hopes about the FUTURE of the child when they grow up are likely her source of Ikigai.

What might be the source of your Ikigai right now?

This book is structured around different age groups, with each chapter representing a season. The Spring chapter features people in their twenties, thirties, and forties, while the Summer chapter focuses on those in their fifties and sixties. The Autumn chapter highlights individuals in their seventies and eighties, and the Winter chapter shares stories from people in their nineties.

We've chosen to link these age groups to the metaphor of Japanese seasons, drawing on the symbolism of each season to reflect the phases of life. Each season represents a unique stage of growth, maturity, reflection, and wisdom, just as the natural world transitions through these cycles.

But as you read, you will feel that 'age is just a number' isn't merely a proverb, and that seasonal ups and downs of life are an annual affair. While you experience journeys of real and ordinary people from Japan, all the way from their twenties to centenarians, no matter whether you're in the Spring, Summer, Autumn, or Winter stage of your life, their stories would definitely inspire you and others you care about.

This book is divided into two parts:

- Part One: 'Stories' showcases remarkable individuals from Japan living a life of Ikigai.
- Part Two: 'myIkigai365 Nourishment Journal' is a carefully curated collection of tools to support you on your own Ikigai journey.

This structure is designed to support your ability to relish it at your own pace—whether in a single sitting or as a reference journal. The essence of the uniquely Japanese word *mypace*—referring to someone who does things at their own pace, in their own way, regardless of outside pressure or expectations—is an integral part of Ikigai journeys, as it combines the physical aspect of speed with the emotional aspect of comfort. Therefore, for some, it means slowing down; for others, it means speeding up; while for a few more, it means an alternating pattern of intensely fast and relaxed slow.

No matter what works best for you, it is this awareness of the pace, and how it makes you feel, combined with feeling in control of the gear that drive this pace, makes it mypace. You can consciously extricate yourself from modes like autopilot, rat-race, hamster-on-a-wheel, and so on.

The stories in Part One of this book are further categorized into stories and short stories. The former provides a detailed narrative enriched with a clinical psychologist's view, practical tools, and reflection exercises to help you take the first step. Some tools are rooted in psychology research, while others are inspired by the natural wisdom of the stories themselves, helping you connect with your emotions. Each tool is designed to encourage meaningful action and deepen your Ikigai experience. While you can explore all the tools over time, we suggest focusing on the story that speaks to you the most right now. After each chapter, we ask that you pause and use the Ikigai365 reflection to start your 'tuning-in' and 'nourishment' of your own Ikigai365 journey.

Additionally, stories feature thoughtfully crafted sidebars to connect Japanese culture and the story's essence, offering refreshing breaks akin to palate cleansers in a multi-course meal.

Short stories, on the other hand, are concise and engaging, perfect for a quick yet impactful read. We're confident you'll enjoy exploring these bite-sized narratives as well.

Reading this book is going to feel like a roller coaster. Meeting some amazing people and hearing their life stories might just give you a whole new way of looking at things. They might even trigger some nostalgia inside you and stir up memories, possibly nudging you to wake up the next day and make that one change which will make you feel good. They might make you reimagine your dreams or help you emerge out of a slump. Whatever form it takes, we sincerely hope it helps you become your own agent of change towards a life of feeling more alive and more fulfilled every day—starting today!

As you read these stories, they could remind you of people in your life whom you admire—perhaps even subconsciously. You might find yourself thinking of an uncle or aunt in your family who has been a real source of inspiration, a role model for you; or a friend who you care deeply about, who stirs up memories or parallels. This might be your chance to reconnect with them, get deeper into their minds, and learn even more from their experiences.

We believe that storytelling is the most effective way to impart lasting and lifelong lessons. That's why, using practical tools and advice, we want to bring to you inspiring stories of Ikigai journeys with minimal theories and models.

As you read on, you might see bits of your own life staring back at you. You might find your dreams, your hopes, and maybe even parts of you that you've kept hidden away. This is a place where it's okay to be real, to think about what matters to you, and to be honest about what you hope to find. We also hope you will notice that everyone has their share of challenges, life's ups and downs, and that no one's life is perfect or fair. We can all draw strength from their own journeys to tune into a wider variety of Ikigai sources.

While we live in a hero/celebrity-worship world, this book hopes your Ikigai journey helps you discover and shape the hero/celebrity that you already are and can become. Over the next pages, we will challenge conventional notions of life stages by promoting the idea of a healthy and fulfilling life every day, regardless of age. Ikigai isn't about life stages; it's about embracing life as an overall stage where individuals feel like standing on their own every day, performing their acts: whether opening a café, dancing, writing a book, or volunteering—to name a few.

This book is like a celebration of the superhero inside you!

But how can we help you on your Ikigai journey?

Maybe you're looking for a reason to get excited about your days, or maybe you've heard about this concept called Ikigai, and you want to know what this is all about. No matter why you're here, this book is full of inspirational stories and reflection tools to help you (re)look closely at your life so far and identify more threads that can help you feel truly alive and fulfilled every day.

Welcome to the exploration of Ikigai, the path you're about to travel. We are honoured to accompany you on this journey.

Let's begin the adventure!

Soredewa . . . Ikigai no tabi e

Onward to a journey of making every day worth living!

History of Ikigai

The origins of Ikigai can be linked to Japan's Heian period (794–1185 AD), where the concept, while not explicitly named, was part of the cultural and philosophical ideas of the time. The Heian period was a significant era in Japanese history, known for its art, poetry, and courtly culture, which collectively strengthened a deep appreciation for aesthetics, nature, and the subtle nuances of life.

As the idea of Ikigai evolved, it was influenced by two major philosophical and religious traditions: Shinto and Confucianism. Shinto, the indigenous spirituality of Japan, emphasizes living harmoniously with nature and finding spiritual energy in everyday life. It encourages individuals to appreciate the present moment and find joy in small, simple pleasures, which aligns with the principles of Ikigai.

Confucianism, introduced to Japan from China, brought with it teachings that stressed the importance of societal harmony, duty, and personal development. It encouraged individuals to find their role in society and fulfil it to the best of their abilities, which resonates with the Ikigai principle of finding purpose and meaning in life.

Buddhism, which began in India, reached Japan in the sixth century, travelling through the Silk Road to China and Korea before crossing the sea to Japan. Buddhism's emphasis on self-reflection aligns with Japan's concept of Ikigai, as both encourage living in the present. Through mindfulness and self-awareness, individuals find inner peace, purpose, and ultimately, enlightenment, also referred to as *nirvana*. Enlightened beings are believed to gain deep compassion, recognizing a unique purpose in their lives.

Interestingly, authors from different cultural backgrounds and different parts of Asia collaborated on the concept of Ikigai in this book. It's a remarkable coincidence that brought us together for this project. Across the continent, societies place great importance on introspection and self-reflection. This shared cultural emphasis led us to Japan, where we discovered Ikigai as a common thread that inspired us to write this book together.

Fast forward to the twenty-first century, and there's been a new wave of excitement about Ikigai. This resurgence can be largely attributed to the influential work of Kamiya Mieko, a prominent Japanese psychiatrist and author, who is often referred to as 'The Mother of Ikigai Psychology', due to her significant contributions to the understanding and popularization of Ikigai.

Through Kamiya Mieko's pioneering work[1], the concept of Ikigai has transcended cultural boundaries, offering a universal framework for achieving a fulfilling and meaningful life in the modern world.

The increase in awareness of Ikigai was significantly fuelled by initiatives such as the National Geographic Blue Zones Project, based on the work of author and researcher Dan Buettner.

His research involved identifying regions around the world where people lived notably longer and healthier lives. These regions, which he termed as Blue Zones, include areas such as Okinawa in Japan, Sardinia in Italy, Nicoya Peninsula in Costa Rica, Ikaria in Greece, and Loma Linda in California. Through his extensive studies, Buettner discovered common lifestyle traits and practices among the inhabitants of these regions that contributed to their exceptional longevity and well-being.

One of the key findings from Buettner's research was the importance of having a sense of purpose. In Okinawa, for instance, the concept of Ikigai was identified as a significant factor in the residents' overall happiness and longevity. By highlighting its role in fostering a fulfilling life, the project has brought increased attention to the concept on a global scale.

Kamiya Mieko, The Mother of Modern Ikigai

As you explore deeper into our book, you'll come across the model known as Three Elements of Ikigai.[2] According to Prof. Hasegawa, who devised it, this model is inspired by the work of Kamiya Mieko (1914–1979), which makes it crucial for us to introduce you to her.

Kamiya Mieko was born in Japan. Her academic journey led her to study medicine and psychiatry, where she developed a deep interest in human psychology and the factors that contribute to a fulfilling life. Her work was influenced by both Western psychological theories and traditional Japanese philosophies.

Mieko was one of the first academics to extensively study Ikigai. Her groundbreaking book from 1966, *Ikigai Ni Tsuite* (About Ikigai), is still considered a standard reference by contemporary Japanese researchers, professors, and psychologists, despite it being published over half-a-century ago.

Her book delves deeply into the concept, exploring how individuals can find both purpose and happiness in their lives. Mieko emphasizes that Ikigai is more than just a fleeting sense of pleasure or a superficial goal: It is a profound sense of meaning and fulfilment that arises from engaging in activities that resonate with one's inner self.

She thus proposed a comprehensive approach to understanding and experiencing Ikigai by combining two essential components:

1. Identifying the source of Ikigai
2. Experiencing the feeling of Ikigai

She also suggested adopting seven specific mindsets to effectively search for both its source and feelings. These mindsets provide a framework for understanding and integrating it into daily life, ensuring a holistic and fulfilling approach:

1. Satisfaction and fulfilment in life
2. Curiosity of change and growth
3. Hope in brighter future
4. Resonating connection with others
5. Freedom
6. Self-actualization
7. Meaning and value

Kamiya Mieko has not only been an inspiration, but also a guiding figure in our journey to explore Ikigai. We'd like to give a heartfelt tribute to her incredible insights which have inspired us to write this book and share the journey of finding joy and purpose with you all.

Three Elements of Ikigai Model and Ikigai365 Framework

Prof. Akihiro Hasegawa's journey with Ikigai started over twenty years ago, back when he chose the theme of his doctoral programme inspired by the clinical practice of dementia, as well as Kamiya Mieko's seminal work. Based off her model, Prof. Hasegawa devised one that hypothesized the structure of Ikigai to include the concept of 'Self as Agent', which is at the overlap of Mieko's concept of Sources and Feelings of Ikigai.[3]

Three Elements of Ikigai Model

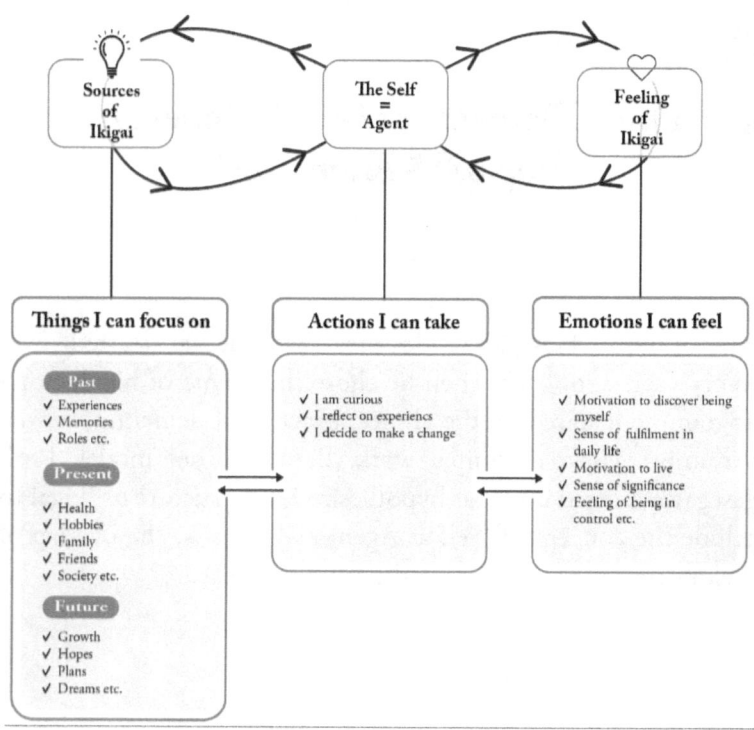

While his research focused on the elderly, it not only established regional differences in the feeling of Ikigai, but also confirmed its hypothesized structure of with statistically robust empirical data.[4]

One qualitative story he often shares to better explain the structure of Ikigai is rooted in his own Three Elements of Ikigai model, wherein he observed differences in dementia patients. During cold winters in the northern parts of Japan, people were often confined to their homes leading to significantly reduced social interactions and stimuli—both critical triggers behind sources and feelings of Ikigai.

He observed that while most patients found their dementia had worsened, only some maintained it—the key factor being that they gave themselves a reason to wake up every morning: watering their plants, going to the nearby grocery store where they would interact with others were some instances.

To make this model more accessible and intuitive to put into everyday practice, Ikigai365 was first created by two of the co-authors of this book, Prof. Hasegawa and Shivendu Nadkarni, in the year 2019. It spotlights a few key aspects from the former's Three Elements of Ikigai model that can help demystify the true meaning of Ikigai, providing a practical way of embracing its authentic journeys for all.

Before you proceed, further, a few points to note:

Remember, Ikigai is your own personal journey. It's not a destination you go in search of. There is no answer or model or algorithm that will magically transform your life.

Authentic Ikigai journeys also flow from everyday life experiences—not the pursuit of big dreams or destinations, rather small achievements that trigger different feelings originating from within you.

The seeds of Ikigai are all around you. They show up in various forms, both external stimuli as well as internal thoughts. Ikigai365, however, is about developing your ability to tune into these regularly.

Ikigai is not a bed of roses. It is not the pursuit of happiness, nor a path to nirvana; rather, it involves embracing the roller-coaster of everyday emotions—both positive and negative. It is also important to tune-in and understand the triggers of both these emotions—an everyday nourishment practice that improves the journey over time.

The Ikigai journey is about unshackling the present self so that it can become the agent of change to make your life worth living every day. Over time, it helps release you from the clutches of your past self (too much of which leads to recurring negative emotions—especially sadness and anger—and associated depressing thoughts) as well as the future self (too much of which leads to recurring negative emotions—especially fear—and associated anxious thoughts).

So, we leave you with two simple questions that you can ask yourself everyday to keep fine-tuning your own sources of Ikigai and nourishing your journey towards it:

1. What (all) makes you feel alive, that you look forward to in the day when you wake up in the morning?
2. What (all) makes you feel fulfilled, that you 'look forward to again tomorrow', when you lie down to go to sleep at night?

Ikigai365 Framework

Part 1

Stories

Chapter 1 – Spring

Spring, the season of hope, new beginnings, and transformation, fuelled by youthful zest, is a chance to start fresh—a light after the long, cold winter, reminding us that every ending carries the seed of a new beginning.

The stories in this chapter—covering people in their twenties, thirties, and forties—welcome new thinking, breaking free from old patterns, just like spring follows winter, allowing the old to give way to the new!

Life Worth ≠ Net Worth

Meet Fujio-san.

Life's secret mantra: 'Small happiness leads to big happiness in life. So, instead of chasing big achievements, celebrate the small ones that lead to fulfilment in life.'

Fujio Kojima, a curious and determined individual, has dedicated his life to solving the world's environmental problems, with a particular focus on waste management.

Do you think he was always this way, or did he do something in his childhood that planted this seed in him?

Let's explore his story and uncover what led him down this path.

As a young kid, Fujio-san was inspired by superheroes, who were always solving peoples' problems, something he found very inspirational.

Then, at the age of seven, he came across a series of book called *Environmental Issues of the World*, each volume of which covered one of the seven major environmental issues. This book, he believes, changed his life.

When he thought about what a hero is supposed to be, he realized that it's not just about being strong or cool, but about fighting against significant problems. At that time, environmental issues seemed overwhelmingly important to him, and because the enemy was big and challenging, he felt a sense of urgency.

Fujio-san told us that the more he read about the issue, the more serious—and fascinating—it became. He also began to feel anxious, worrying that someone else might solve the problem before he was old enough to do it by himself! So, he kept borrowing the same book from the library over and over again, hoping to keep the idea of solving this problem to himself.

As he grew older and entered his teenage years, life brought new priorities—one such being the desire to have a girlfriend. He figured his chances might improve if he took up tennis. Though he knew he'd never be great at the game, he continued to enjoy playing it.

During this period, he also began volunteering as a ball boy on tennis courts, where he came face-to-face with some of the sport's biggest idols. But off the court, he saw a different side to them, realizing how unhappy these players were. He saw players storming back in the locker room after losing a game, smashing their racket against the wall, and yelling that they hated this game. He also noticed that the winners' high did not last long. Soon enough, they would start thinking about winning the next game. Such incidents burst his bubble.

He had always believed that success and happiness are somehow interlinked, but now he found there was no correlation between them. Instead, he realized that joy came from the small victories: of winning each point, pushing through the grunts and sweat.

As Fujio-san pursued his education, he enrolled at Osaka Prefectural University, hoping to solve environmental issues as a researcher who could tackle environment issues. But in his fourth year, when he was assigned to a research lab, he began to question whether this path was right for him. He realized that academic research often involves dedicating your whole life to a single theme, whose research output rarely dealt into practical situations. It was more about studying the problems than solving them.

He had two choices: join a company or start one. Instead of picking just one, he decided to try both. But first, he chose to attend graduate school and worked hard to get into Kyoto University.

While in college, he shared his dream of solving environmental issues with an Indian friend. His friend responded, 'Living in Osaka, you won't truly understand what an environmental problem is. You should experience a place where the pollution is so severe that you can't take a deep breath.' These words deeply impacted Fujio-san, making him realize that that to make a real difference, he needed first-hand experience in a developing country.

So, he took a two-year break and moved to Vietnam, working as a salesman to understand the life of a corporate employee. Yet, he still struggled to pinpoint which specific environmental issue he wanted to tackle. Hoping for clarity, and to witness the challenges firsthand, he decided to travel the world. He was twenty-three at the time.

To fund his travels, he worked a variety of part-time jobs, saving every penny. Over the course of three months, he explored different regions, including the depths of the Amazon rainforest. There, he saw massive deforestation—and a surprising revelation. Locals had cleared an area of dense forest to create a football field. He realized that people everywhere, even in the heart of the jungle, aspired to the conveniences and opportunities of modern life. The drive for development, he concluded, posed a greater threat to the planet than the wild animals ever could. This insight reignited his childhood determination to tackle environmental challenges.

Throughout his journey, Fujio-san encountered countless eye-opening experiences in both developed and developing nations. He witnessed the devastating effects of waste and pollution, experiences that only deepened his conviction and strengthened his resolve to find practical, effective solutions for the planet's most urgent environmental problems.

During his travels, Fujio-san came up with around hundred ideas to pursue, one of which focused on tackling littering.

He initially believed that a sudden moment of inspiration—like a lightning bolt—would reveal the perfect idea. But that moment never came.

On the flight back home, he panicked. He had spent all his time and money on the trip, yet he hadn't settled on a concrete idea. Returning to Japan, some personal circumstances added to his desperation and impatience, pushing him to forcefully connect the ideas that seemed promising in his notebook.

However, he faced financial constraints that made it difficult to launch his initiatives. Undeterred, he made significant personal sacrifices, including moving into a tiny apartment that doubled as his office. This allowed him to conserve funds and kickstart his work.

Inspired by the prevalent issue of littering in every city visited, Fujio-san founded Pirika Inc. in November 2011. The word *pirika* means 'beautiful' in Ainu language, spoken by the indigenous people of Japan.

Fujio-san believes that while humans are the cause of their own problems, they are also the solution. He is convinced that everyone wants to make a difference, given an opportunity.

Pirika is a free social networking service (SNS) app that encourages litter-picking activities, where users can post photos of and comment on the litter they pick up. Think of it as the X (formerly Twitter) or Facebook for litter picking! But instead of the usual 'likes' there's a 'thank you' button to express gratitude. Through this app, Pirika aims to maximize the number of people picking up litter and the amount of litter collected. To date, the app has collected over 335 million pieces of litter in 126 countries and received several prestigious awards in Japan and abroad.

Starting Pirika was not that easy for Fujio-san. He also faced his share of challenges, but what he learned from his time on the tennis court—'to be more sensitive to small successes'—helped him a lot. He recalls when he launched the test app, only hundred people downloaded it, and only five of them picked up the trash. Normally, these numbers might seem like a failure, and he would have given up, but he saw potential. 100 strangers downloaded the app, and 5 per cent of them took action to pick up trash, without any incentives. He further notes that the test app was so badly designed that even a 0 per cent would've been unsurprising, but 5 per cent seemed amazing. It made him realize that with serious improvements to the design and features, there was a possibility that he could pick up trash around the world through the app.

Before starting Pirika, Fujio-san read many books on entrepreneurship and the stories of success and failure, always wondering why people give up. He was always aware of this and found ways to inspire himself to keep going.

He says that his parents and friends always supported him during his journey—and honestly, they believed in him more than he believed in himself. He always thought, 'I can't disappoint my loved ones for their faith in me,' and this was his driver to keep going during the challenging phases.

He also considered that if he gave up on his company, he would have to work for someone else, and he didn't like the idea of working under a boss, so he had no choice but to keep going.

Reflecting on what he has learned from his own mistakes, Fujio-san says, 'We need to be kinder to each other and appreciate each other's diversity.' He adds, 'My younger brother and I were always different in our likes and interests, and I was fairly intolerant of those differences as a child. Now I realize that everyone has unique skills. My younger brother has great communication skills and is very good at making friends, while I'm passionate about learning and solving problems. Now, I can respect these differences.'

Continuing his entrepreneurial journey, Fujio-san and his team also developed an artificial intelligence (AI) system capable of scanning streets for garbage, streamlining waste collection processes, and enhancing efficiency. Additionally, he initiated a comprehensive project surveying plastic waste in rivers and coastal areas across Japan. This project raised awareness about the devastating impact of plastic pollution on the environment while also identifying critical areas for targeted intervention.

Fujio-san's company remains at the forefront of innovation, constantly exploring new technologies and approaches to address waste management challenges. His unwavering determination, passion, and ability to leverage IT solutions have positioned him as a pioneer in the field. Through his tireless efforts, Fujio-san is actively working toward a cleaner, more sustainable future, demonstrating that individuals with vision and dedication can make a profound impact on the world's environmental challenges.

When we met him, we asked how fulfilled he felt in his life. He replied, 'I am satisfied with my family and work life. I really disconnect from everything when I go home to my wife and two kids. When I return to work, I keep looking to learn new things and don't allow myself to get too comfortable. I want to keep challenging myself all the time.'

We also asked him how he balances money and purpose, and whether he believes he is living his Ikigai.

He responded that he does indeed believe he is living his Ikigai. 'I feel fulfilled and happy doing what I am doing,' he said. 'I didn't care about money as such; I focused on doing my job and making an impact on waste management issues.' He went on to add, 'Pirika is my "Ikigai" not "Hatarakigai". Money is not my only driving force. Even if I wasn't getting paid for it, I would still be doing this.'

Please read the Sidebar 'Ikigai > Hatarakigai' on page no. 15 to get more details about Hatarakigai.

Here is a glimpse of few more questions we asked him during the interview:

Q. How was Pirika born, and how is it making a difference to the world?

An insight that motivates me to do more is that everyone wants to make a difference. I believe that while humans are the cause of their own problems, they are also the solution. Given an opportunity, everyone wants to make a difference.

Pirika is an app that promotes litter-picking by allowing users to share photos and comments about the trash they collect. It's like a social network for cleaning up the environment.

We looked to make an app that was very simple, where everyone had an opportunity to be a part of it and thereby making a difference to the world.

This model worked and now we work with several municipalities in the collection of garbage for them.

Q. What next?

Ideally, we would like to go for an IPO to be able to raise capital and go global. We have started with waste, and going forward, we want to focus on other environmental issues like air and water.

Q. How do you balance money and purpose? Do you believe you are living your Ikigai?

I do believe I am living my Ikigai. I feel fulfilled and happy doing what I am doing.

I didn't care about money as such: I'm focused on doing my job and making an impact on waste management issues. Going forward, we may need to get some customers to pay for the service, but we will cross that bridge when we come to it.

Q. How do you know Pirika is your Ikigai (reason to live) and not your Hatarakigai (reason to work)?

Yes, Pirika is my Ikigai. It is my passion and my biggest challenge. It also makes me some money, and I'm happy doing what I am doing. Money isn't my only driving force.

Even if I was not getting paid, I would still be doing this. So, I am sure this is my Ikigai and not my Hatarakigai.

Q. What would be your advice to young children?

Advice is something that can be given or appreciated only if someone really wants it. And sometimes, we believe the advice from our parents and teachers is outdated.

As for me, I truly went ahead and did what I always wanted to do as a child. While my loved ones support me, they don't quite understand what and why I do what I'm doing. Had I become a scientist, I would not have been happy writing research papers on global issues alone; I am a person who needs to go out and solve things by myself. This is why I think I was always cut out to be an entrepreneur. Moreover, there were no jobs in this space I operate from, so I had no other choice either.

We are always trying to be the person our parents or our friends want, and it may not always be productive or good for what we are truly passionate about.

My advice for parents, however, is to understand that your children are unlike you. Let them follow their dreams, so more passion ventures like Pirika can be created.

Soon, Fujio-san seeks out permission to express something. 'I was very reluctant to do this interview initially,' he says.

'But why?' we ask.

'I feel I have not reached a stage in life where I can teach people,' he says. 'I have even seen those who have reached the top of their professional lives fade away into oblivion after their books and interviews emerged.'

This is followed by a question. 'I want to know why you chose me for this interview?'

We express that our book is about everyday heroes at home and work, including housewives, nurses, retirees, and entrepreneurs. We are not looking for conventional success stories, but, in fact, people who have worked on their minds to create a life of fulfilment in whatever situation they are in—those who have demonstrated action towards their thinking and beliefs and have made an impact on themselves and their ecosystem.

Now, Fujio-san is the one asking questions, and we, the authors, are answering them.

Q. What's the difference between people who try hard and who have given up?

Look at, for example, Ogawa-san (who appears later in the book, in the Winter chapter), who is already a centenarian, and hasn't yet given up learning and growing. She is still acting on what she believes in: She conceived a book at the age of ninety, and now, at hundred, Ogawa-san is one of the oldest authors in the world. We intend to cover such stories of inspiration about never giving up.

People are doing these things because, likely, it's their Ikigai. If someone is working only to make money, then in a challenging situation, a person may give up.

Prof. Hasegawa's Ikigai Expert Commentary

When I read Fujio-san's story, it immediately struck me that he started his own business to solve environmental problems, something he was strongly influenced for at a very young age of seven by reading books on environmental issues. As he grew up, he continued learning by traveling around the world in his youth to understand more about the current state of the environment.

Now, in his professional life, his corporate philosophy is to simply improve the environment and manage waste rather than to try to earn huge amounts of money, which gives him a strong sense of fulfilment and accomplishment. Even when he encounters difficult situations, he discovers small joys around him and stays motivated by the feeling that comes from within to accomplish his activities. Fujio-san also appears to continuously expand his imagination and deepen his thinking through reading and experimenting. This helps fuel his curiosity and reduce his worry and anxiety.

Psychologist Edward Deci emphasized that intrinsic motivation—driven by personal growth, passion, and meaning—is more strongly associated with happiness than extrinsic rewards like money or fame.[5]

Achieving success for external validation might feel hollow, while pursuing internal goals often leads to a deeper sense of fulfilment.[6]

Ikigai is a feeling that originates from within—maybe as an emotion that then manifests into motivation to make your life worth living. This is different from Hatarakigai, and you can recognize these as external sources of motivation like money, position, etc. Your sources of Ikigai primarily come from inside of you and are unique to your own life experiences.

Heartfelt advice from Fujio-san

How do you know what you are doing is your Ikigai and not your Hatarakigai?

You will know because you will still be doing it, even if you were not getting paid for it.

So, find your Ikigai, and don't confuse it with your Hatarakigai. Even if I was not getting paid, I would still be doing this. So, this is my Ikigai, and not Hatarakigai.

We hope that you enjoyed Fujio-san's story, and that it triggered some feelings inside you. Allow us to give you a tiny nudge here and now for your own Ikigai365 journey.

Close your eyes and take a deep breath, reflecting on the following questions before writing down the answer:

At work, or in life, what makes me feel most alive and fulfilled is

_____

_____

_____

Would you still do it, if you were not paid, recognized, or rewarded for this?

_____

In the myIkigai365 Nourishment Journal on page 229, you may wish to use the tool 'Ikigai > Hatarakigai'.

If Fujio-san can, so can you. Take that first step today!

Sidebar: Ikigai (life worth living) and Hatarakigai (work worth doing)

What if you realized that your own sources of Ikigai are not only meaningful but also powerful sources of daily energy? Energy that sparks your sense of being alive, as well as feeling fulfilled! This creates a virtuous cycle that you look forward to experiencing every single day, without needing to be paid or expecting any recognition for it.

Hataraku means to work, so Hatarakigai (働きがい) refers to the sense that one's work is worth 'doing'—often resulting in feelings of success, achievement, and reward. This concept is typically tied to professional activities where rewards are monetary.

On the other hand, Ikiru means to live, and Ikigai (生き甲斐) refers to the sense that life itself is worth 'living,' bringing a sense of belonging, being alive in the moment, and overall fulfilment. Ikigai applies to everyone, every day, and the rewards here are emotional rather than financial.

Looking at the broader picture, nearly half the global population isn't employed—including children, students, retirees, homemakers, etc. These individuals derive their sense of worth from various sources and experiences unrelated to the professional world or money. For them, Hatarakigai may not always apply in daily life, even though they might encounter it in relation to their past or future.

But still, everyone deserves to wake up every morning looking forward to spending the day feeling alive and fulfilled—regardless of whether they are professionally employed or financially rewarded.

While questions around work, career, passion, vocation, expertise, and, of course, money, can help navigate the competitive and fast-evolving professional world, they are not the only measures of fulfilment. The good news is that as work and career paths become more complex, there's a growing interest in using the concept of Hatarakigai to make workplaces more attractive to future employees and strengthen environments that foster employee satisfaction and retention.

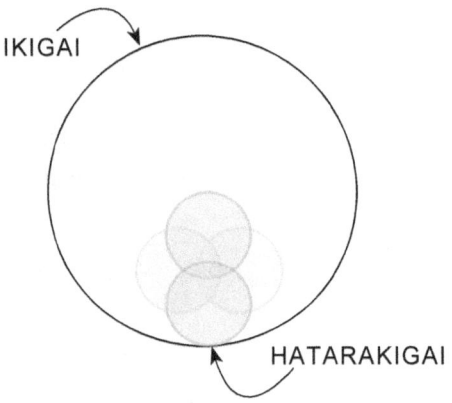

Ikigai > Hatarakigai

But life is much bigger and broader than work. When we think about our lives in the broadest psychological terms, we humans have an ever-changing and continuously evolving sense of identity that is closely linked to our sense of control (e.g. achievements, roles, and responsibilities) as well as our sense of belonging (e.g. family, friends, interest groups, etc.).

The Three Elements of Ikigai Model reinforces that these and other senses are manifested every day as emotions—regardless of whether we consciously tune into them or acknowledge our feelings.

- These emotions that we experience as feelings make us 'feel alive'.
- The daily emotional roller-coaster of both positive and negative emotions makes us 'feel human'.
- These emotions are triggered by both internal thoughts and external people and events.

> - These emotions are associated with past experiences, present realities, and future expectations.
>
> *Go to tool 'Ikigai > Hatarakigai' on Page 229 to engage in a deeper self-reflection and discover your own sources of Ikigai.*

Key quote

'One moment can change a day, one day can change a life, and one life can change the world'

—Buddha

Connections that Celebrate Generations

Meet Hamano-san.

Life's secret mantra: 'Belonging is not just a place. It's a feeling of being needed, valued, and seen.'

Masayuki Hamano, a thirty-one-year-old occupational therapist, is on a mission to combat the isolation and loneliness experienced by the elderly and creating a space for the young and old where they belong. What sets his initiative apart is not only its social impact, but also its innovative for-profit business model.

As a fresh graduate, Hamano-san began his career as an occupational therapist, visiting the homes of people with disabilities. He also initiated and volunteered in activities aimed at connecting the elderly with children. It was during one such activity that he had a life-altering encounter. An elderly lady, who wasn't covered by insurance, shared with him, 'I am very lonely, and there's no one to talk to, so even once a week is fine. Can you please call me? I would like to talk to someone at least once in a while.'

These words left a profound impact on him. He realized that many elderly individuals were suffering from loneliness and isolation in their homes. However, the insurance system only covered such people once they had deteriorated to a point where they were already ill. This prompted him to think beyond the constraints of the system, leading to the birth of Engao—a place where people, specially seniors, can be themselves, feel valued, and connect through mutual support and understanding.

Hamano-san's inspiration for creating Engao was also influenced by his experiences as a volunteer in the aftermath of the Tohoku earthquake in Japan, and his international volunteer work in countries like Cambodia and the Philippines. It taught him the importance of genuinely understanding the needs of the people and developing sustainable plans to meet those needs.

In 2017, at the age of twenty-five, Hamano-san utilized abandoned *akiya* houses in his community to create Engao. Initially, it was a place for elderly individuals to gather and spend time together. Hamano-san firmly believes that everyone, young or old, needs a sense of ibasho—a place where you feel you belong or can be yourself. Its concept transcends physical abilities; even those with limitations experience a profound sense of belonging and presence.

Engao became that place where the elderly could mingle and connect with young volunteers. Slowly, it evolved into a hub for various activities, where older individuals shared their skills and knowledge with the younger generation and vice versa.

He also established a homework club for children on the second floor of the facility, allowing them to interact with the elderly. Parents would drop off and pick up their children, fostering conversations between different generations. In a neighbouring building, Hamano-san created a shared house where both young and old residents lived together. Additionally, he established a community café, as well as a home for the disabled and mentally challenged, along a daycare facility for very young children—all within close proximity.

Hamano-san's work extends beyond just creating meeting places for the elderly. He aims to provide an environment where they feel needed, useful, and genuinely cared for. With a commitment to build a truly inclusive and supportive community at Engao, Hamano-san introduced several thoughtful initiatives that go beyond conventional care.

One example is the *ashiyu*, a soothing hot tub designed for individuals to soak their tired legs. This feature, strategically positioned outside the childcare area, serves multiple purposes: It offers elderly visitors a place to relax and observe children at play, creating a heart-warming atmosphere for intergenerational interaction. Moreover, it provides parents dropping off their kids a chance to engage in conversation, share their challenges, and form meaningful connections with others facing similar situations.

Hamano-san's mission goes beyond the physical amenities he has put in place. He is driven by a deep understanding of the emotional well-being of both the elderly and the wider community. His determination to create Engao was further fuelled when he came across a newspaper article reporting that a staggering 60 per cent of suicides in Japan, spanning across different age groups, occur with reasons that remain unknown. This shocking revelation underscored the acute need for individuals to have someone to confide in, share their struggles, and seek help during challenging times.

He observed adults in Japan are reluctant to seek assistance or express their emotions driven by the cultural aversion to appearing weak or imperfect. He further felt that many adults in the country feel that revealing their vulnerabilities or shortcomings is a sign of weakness, choosing instead to present only their perfected selves to the world. This tendency to suppress emotions and struggles and the pressure to maintain an image of strength, inevitably leads to heightened stress levels among the adult population.

Remarkably, the repercussions of this culture extended to the younger generation, as children mirrored these behaviours and adopted a similar approach. The children growing up in this environment internalize these expectations, learning to suppress their emotions. The Japanese term *gaman*, which translates to 'endure' or 'hold it up', was frequently imparted to children by their parents, reinforcing the notion that showing vulnerability is undesirable.

At Engao, he aspires to create a space where the elderly can feel safe and comfortable asking for help, admitting failures without the fear of judgment, thereby demonstrating to younger generations the importance of seeking help when needed and acknowledging one's flaws is a natural part of life. Engao strives to be a place where individuals can be unapologetically themselves, where the community celebrates each person's unique attributes, fostering an environment of mutual support, acceptance, and genuine connection.

Also, by focusing on his own self-care and happiness, Hamano-san ensures that both his team and volunteers maintain a positive outlook. This approach, where happiness begets happiness, creates a virtuous cycle benefiting the elderly, volunteers, and the broader community. He truly believes that the key to creating successful communities lies in the happiness of those who run them.

Hamano-san creates a cycle of positivity by placing joy and emotional well-being at the centre of Engao's work. Instead of rushing to meet every need, the team first asks, 'Can we enjoy doing this?' thus ensuring their efforts remain sustainable and fulfilling. This mindset encourages rest, emotional check-ins, and mutual support, helping prevent burnout. Everyone at Engao—regardless of role—is seen as both a giver and receiver of care, building a balanced, respectful community. Daily self-reflection is encouraged as a form of self-care, fostering clarity and presence. For Hamano-san, happiness isn't the outcome—it's the energy that powers lasting impact.

His philosophy is rooted in the belief that the work itself should be enjoyable and fulfilling, marking the first measure of success. If the participants are happy, it's an added success, and if the endeavour becomes financially sustainable, that's a bonus. The secret lies in having fun and ensuring that the community meets genuine needs.

Today, Engao touches the lives of over 1,000 young volunteers annually, fostering a nurturing atmosphere that inspires continued volunteering. Engao utilizes seven abandoned houses, all located within a two-minute walk from each other, to operate a diverse array of facilities. These include elderly salons, children's spaces, community cafeterias, share houses, group homes for individuals with disabilities, co-working spaces, and a home school for children who cannot cope with regular ones. His team also visits homes of the elderly who cannot commute and help them with their daily needs. In his unique approach to community building, Hamano-san emphasizes that it's not merely about providing a meeting place for the elderly. Instead, he believes that people should feel needed and should have a role to play, a sense of purpose, making the space truly their own.

What sets Engao apart is its innovative for-profit business model that offers services like childcare and co-working spaces to parents, ensuring that the elderly are not burdened financially. Engao keeps operational costs minimal by utilizing abandoned homes and avoiding extravagant spending on the interiors. This approach creates a homely atmosphere for the elderly, contributing to their sense of comfort and belonging. Ultimately, Hamano-san envisions Engao as a place where individuals can be themselves, free from the pressure to constantly present their best selves to the world.

Prof. Hasegawa's Ikigai Expert Commentary

People are born alone in the world. And they die alone. However, while people are alive, they meet others and form connections. When one no longer feels 'connection' with others, it leads to isolation. Solitude has a will, but isolation does not.

Hamano-san felt very helpless after the Great East Japan earthquake. He was moved deeply by the shock of loneliness in the aftermath of the natural disaster. He also felt pained and helpless when he was training to become an Occupational Therapist after noticing that the system was not providing the care needed to prevent the widespread loneliness experienced by the seniors. He channelled that into starting up a non-profit organization that used available resources (both physical and human) to create mutual symbiosis—sometime unexpectedly.

At Engao, Hamano-san tried to create a mechanism to prevent people from becoming isolated—a system that respects the will that is in solitude, but trying to avoid isolation. He created opportunities and places for people to connect with each other across generations: not alone, but with his friends; not as a single charismatic figure, but by facing and discussing with everyone.

Abraham Maslow's Hierarchy of Needs proposes that social connections are a fundamental human need, positioned just above basic survival needs like food, shelter, and safety.[7]

Feelings of belonging and love are necessary for self-actualization and achieving one's potential—once the basic needs are taken care of. Social interactions, hence, become the bedrock of mental and emotional well-being and prevention of chronic isolation. More recently, this is further evidenced in the Kipling Williams' Cyberball Experiment, where participants excluded even from a virtual ball-tossing game experienced feelings of rejection and sadness, demonstrating the psychological effects of social exclusion—not just physical isolation.[8]

Our (self as agent) interactions with the outside world (triggers or people) can either make us feel good or bring us down. When your life experiences involve setbacks or frustrations, try linking them to your own aspirations and achieving your potential. In Hamano's case, this helped him choose his professional path linked to 'giving care' in a way that reduces loneliness. Along the way, he created unexpected ways to improve connections across generations, making everyone involved feel alive and fulfilled in their respective Ikigai journeys.

Heartfelt advice for you, from Hamano-san

Let's all make the world a warmer place by creating 'small connections with each other'. These small acts of kindness can spark a chain reaction that can make people feel less lonely and isolated.

We hope that you enjoyed Hamano-san's story and that it triggered some feelings inside you. Allow us to give you a tiny nudge here-and-now for your own Ikigai365 journey.

Close your eyes and take a deep breath, reflecting on the following questions before writing down the answers:

List a few people and places that make you feel safe, foster a sense of belonging, and allow you to be yourself, free of judgement.

_____

_____

_____

In a week, how often do you spend time at these places and with these people?

_____

If Hamano-san can, so can you. Take that first step today!

Sidebar: Reviving Akiya and Ikigai roots in ancestry

A recent report by Japan's Internal Affairs Ministry revealed that over 9 million homes nationwide are vacant, making up 13.8 per cent of all residential properties.[9]

These abandoned houses, known as akiya, are often left to deteriorate as their elderly owners pass away, move into retirement homes, or due to the burden of high inheritance taxes. This is also because of Japan's population decline.[10]

Startups like Engao represent a potential entrepreneurial or CSR opportunity.

We leave you with a question: Could your Ikigai be linked to your roots and what you want to do for your ancestral place? Think about it.

Key quote

'Belonging is the opposite of loneliness. It's when you find those who understand you and where you feel safe to be yourself.'

—Vironika Tugaleva

Feeling Alive Here-And-Now =
Life Without Regrets

Meet Koko-san.

Life's secret mantra: 'Live a regret-free life and do all the things you want to before you die.'

As we enter Zuma, the famous Japanese restaurant in Madrid, a very sprightly, bright eyed, smiling lady comes to take our order.

'Are you from Japan?' we ask her, and she perks up to vociferously say yes. This sparks a little conversation, and we compliment her. 'You have a very graceful walk.'

She pauses for a minute, smiles, then tells us, 'You know, I used to be a ballet dancer.' There is a sudden change of energy, as if this conversation has taken her down the memory lane.

Koko-san is a young waitress, who came to Europe from Japan to be a professional ballet dancer. What's the story here?

'Is ballet dance your Ikigai?' we ask her.

With abundant clarity, she replies, 'No, my Ikigai is to be happy in the moment, and I am quite happy in my life at this point.'

This conversation was enough for us to ask this question. 'Can we interview you for our Ikigai book?'

She agrees, and we part ways.

Soon, we text her on Instagram for an interview, but don't hear back. *Maybe we should have taken her number*, we think, as she doesn't seem to be active much on that app.

But Koko-san's story continues to linger on our minds. Why must she have given up ballet dance? Such thoughts keep coming in our mind.

A couple of months later, a friend mentions they will be traveling to Madrid, and that they will be dining at Zuma. Immediately, we request them to connect with Koko-san and inform her that we have been trying to get in touch with her.

A week later, we meet her for an interview on Zoom. And she was bright and poignant as ever.

Now, her story.

Born as Kozue Tahiro in a small Japanese town, Koko-san travelled to Germany to pursue a professional career in ballet dancing. She had been learning ballet since the age of five, and at sixteen, she decided she needed to move out of Japan, if this art was to be pursued beyond a hobby. She received a scholarship from Hamburg Ballet School, and that took her to Europe for the first time to live abroad. There, her ballet teacher changed her name to Koko, which remains her European moniker till date.

Practising ballet at school for two years and working as a professional outside of Japan was not easy for a teenager.

After three years in Germany, she got injured and had to return to Japan. When she arrived, she had been depressed, so much so that she was unable to dance—and that was all she had done since the age of five. For six months, she was at home without doing anything. In fact, she hardly stepped out. She was absent-minded, often forgetting what she was thinking mere minutes ago. So much so that one day, she went for a walk and ended up very far away. She had to call her mom, who came to pick her up from the roadside. The mental agony was unbearable.

But one day, her ballet teacher, who lived in the same town as her, called her mother. Together, they reached out to Koko-san. 'You are too talented to give up dancing,' she said. 'And dancing is something which stimulates your soul, you have to start again.' She tried to convince Koko-san.

This was an important trigger for Koko-san to gather herself back up on her feet. She decided to return to her childhood dance school in her hometown. On the very first day, all her childhood memories came flashing back. Getting back into her ballet dress, doing her shoes again, all of it was therapeutic. Though her body didn't move on the first day, she felt happy inside. From that day on, her dream came alive again.

In Japan, one has to pay to go to ballet school. In Europe, on the other hand, it's a respected profession, where one gets paid to be a ballet artist. Before returning to Spain, Koko-san did a month-long tour across Europe. She worked really hard, all motivated, arriving early morning in the class to practice.

But soon, her drive turned into disappointment, as she saw the director favoured a student who would come late, throw attitude, and chew gum standing in the front row of the class. *This isn't fair*, Koko-san felt.

Suddenly, there was a streak of realization. *Ballet's role in my life was to help me back on my feet. This isn't a profession I wish to pursue*, she thought. 'I will practise ballet when I have my own studio in the house. I will dance for myself and my own happiness only.'

And until then, she bid goodbye to ballet.

She felt this was her moment of liberation. 'I could be anything; I felt free. I could breathe the air deeper—I felt happy,' she says. 'I chose to live in Spain because I love the way of life here. Everyone does what they want to do, and everyone expresses themselves as they are and what they feel.'

'Japan is my home country, and I love it for its culture, people, and food,' she says. 'But there, one is expected to follow the norms of the group one is a part of—be it school, ballet group, or the village community. If, at work, the boss invites you for a drink, everyone has to go as a gesture of respect—even if they may be exhausted from the day's work and may wish to return home and sleep. In Spain, however, people express themselves openly, and it is an acceptable norm to say no to your boss, for instance.'

Koko-san says she feels more at home in Spain with the person she is. 'Koko-san, you are beautiful, you don't have to be one track. You can be the best of both,' she had counselled herself saying.

When she was free, she began to share her CV with Japanese restaurants. Soon, she landed a job at a Japanese restaurant, and only six months into the job, she was promoted to the post of manager. This was also the time she learned Spanish.

'My Japanese boss considered working extra hours, without extra pay, to be normal. Being the manager wasn't easy, as I was stuck between my Japanese boss and the Spanish employees who wanted to be paid for the extra time they devoted.'

Thereafter, Koko-san went to work at another Japanese restaurant, where she met the person she was last in a relationship with. However, she had to leave that place, because the boss was unhappy after learning about the relationship between his two workers in the restaurant.

'When my ex-boyfriend went to Zuma for an interview, I waited outside in the street.' But a voice inside Koko-san told her, 'Why don't you introduce yourself to the interviewing team? Maybe, you can work here too.'

She decided to meet the general manager of the cafeteria, who immediately offered her to join—even though she didn't even have her CV with her at the time.

This turned a new leaf in Koko-san's life. Now, she feels accomplished, recognized, and happy.

Koko-san's Interview

Q. **Koko-san, you are brave, adventurous, and you stand for justice. But people with a free mind like you could also face a backlash and be judged by others, who may wonder why you changed so many jobs, and if there was something wrong.**

I have heard the word 'no' so many times in my life. When I was going to ballet, my father never encouraged me, it was with my mom's backing that I continued. My friends always encouraged me to continue, because they felt I had the right body and ankle shape for ballet. 'If we had your body, we would never give up,' they would tell me. But I was always clear after I arrived at my truth: There are better things I am supposed to be doing.

Q. When you hear Ikigai, what comes to your mind?
Do what you like. I want to have a life that I will not regret before I die. My mentality changed after reading the book, *The Top Five Regrets of the Dying* by Bronnie Ware, when I was deep in depression. After reading it, I felt that I should have done what I wanted to do and not have lived my life depending on someone's thoughts. Now, I don't want to have any regrets anymore. I want to do something only because I want to do it.

When I need to decide on something, I should do it only because it makes me excited; not because someone else wants me to do it. I want to live a life that makes me excited—not the one where someone expects me to do something.

When I went to the class, I was thinking how they [the teachers and judges] are looking at me, not how I felt while dancing. I was always scared of being looked at from a casting and performance eye; I was dancing for someone else more than myself. This sucked out the joy from the process. I decided if I want to dance, I will do it only for myself.

For me, dancing was always an expression of my inner self, a feeling that gave me joy. When I worked for the ballet company, I lost that freedom to express my soul and regained it only when I quit ballet.

Q. What is your Ikigai now?

Enjoy what you can do now . . . in this moment. Never say no to anything that comes to you. You never know that it may create a new connection for you.

Q. Do you think your Ikigai will change with time?

For now, this is my Ikigai. But in ten years, it will be different, as it was something else ten years ago as well. Ikigai is something that evolves with the stage, situation, and environment.

Q. What would be your advice for people who are experiencing depression and are unable to break out? What are the steps you took to get out of that situation?

Deep inside, I was ashamed of myself. Even though I had been famous in my small town as that girl who went to Europe for ballet, after I returned, I did not want to be noticed by anyone on the street when I walked around. They knew who I was and thought I had failed in my life. Deep inside, you have to accept who you are, that you failed, that you are not a super hero. Accept who and what you are and then go on.

Secondly, take the first step.

My first step was to go back to ballet.

After that move, it was easy to keep moving, as one thing leads to another—just like it happened in my life.

Prof. Hasegawa's Ikigai Expert Commentary

Koko-san went to Germany from Japan to pursue her future dreams of becoming a ballet dancer. In trying to make her dream a reality, she experienced a strong conflict: Even though she devoted herself to working hard and learning ballet it was difficult, she could not give up because she loved it. As she felt conflicted over time, she gradually wrestled with whether the injury in Hamburg, followed by the unfair episode in Madrid was coincidental or inevitable. Eventually, she acted upon her frustration and gave up learning ballet.

Then, she worked as a manager at a Japanese restaurant in Spain but faced inevitable conflicts and self-doubts. She was worried that her past and present experiences will continue to trouble her in the future. Despite the sense of setback, she successfully shifted her frame of thinking from an 'evaluation of others' to 'self-evaluation', embracing an attitude of trusting her own experiences to be her strength. This further grew into self-confidence as she met and connected with other people while working at the restaurant, and from the support she received and reciprocated with her mother.

Carl Rogers's Self Theory explains how people's emotions are related to their self-concepts and the goals they set for themselves.[11]

Specifically, it states that people compare their actual self to their ideal and ought selves, and that inconsistencies between these can lead to negative emotions. The three domains of self in this theory are Actual Self (who someone is), Ideal Self (who someone wants to be) and Ought Self (who someone thinks others want them to be). The theory associates specific negative emotions, such as fear, disappointment, guilt, and embarrassment, with gaps between a person's actual and ideal selves. It also proposes that people's behaviour is motivated to reduce the discrepancy between their actual and ideal selves.

Koko-san encountered the shock of this gap between her own expectations and actual reality in the ballet world. But her strong will, formed from the years of ballet and combined by the positive memories of it from the past, was channelled by her present. This motivated her to work towards a new future (working at a Japanese restaurant) different from ballet. In doing so, Koko-san had to let go of her ideal future self (professional ballet dancer), and right now, her present self is working hard to recreate a new ideal self of the future, by using all the foundational elements already acquired from ballet.

In the process, she has also clearly learned to let go of others' expectations—this also releases her of a range of associated negative feelings, like regret, for instance.

Now, as a restaurant manager, she is still a work-in-progress, striving towards defining her new ideal self, which she still wants to connect to her earlier ballet dream of setting up a ballet school in the future. It takes a lot of courage and determination for a person to go abroad, learn an art form, and perform in front of people. It's so beautiful to see people like her walk step by step through various experiences in their irreplaceable life and make their Ikigai journeys personal and authentic.

Heartfelt advice for you from Koko-san

Never say no to something that comes to you.

Deep inside you have to accept who you are, that you failed and it's okay if you are not a superhero. Accept who and what you are and then go on. Take the first step!

We hope that you enjoyed Koko-san's story, and that it triggered some feelings inside you.

Allow us to give you a tiny nudge here and now for your own Ikigai365 journey.

Close your eyes and take a deep breath, reflecting on the following questions before writing down the answers:

When you were younger, what were some of your dreams?

_____

_____

_____

Is there a current dream that you are not pursuing, which you might regret later?

_____

If Koko-san can, so can you. Take that first step today!

Sidebar: The Top Five Regrets of the Dying

Bronnie Ware, in her book, *The Top Five Regrets of the Dying*, shares life lessons learned from patients in palliative care. Based on her experience as a nurse, Ware highlights the most common regrets people express before dying:

1. I wish I'd lived true to myself, not what others expected.
2. I wish I hadn't worked so hard.
3. I wish I had expressed my feelings.
4. I wish I'd stayed in touch with my friends.
5. I wish I had allowed myself to be happier

Key quote

'We all have two lives. The second one starts when we realize we only have one.'

—Confucius

Short Story

True Caring = Guilt-free Self-Care

Meet Yumi-San.

As a single child, Yumi-san shoulders the sole responsibility of caring for her aging parents. She finds herself facing numerous challenges as a caregiver. To make matters worse, her husband has recently been diagnosed with a rare disease, further burdening her caregiving duties. Regrettably, neither her parents nor her husband fully acknowledge or appreciate her tireless efforts. Her parents' battle with dementia means they often forget her acts of kindness and tend to complain.

During her father's recent hospitalization, Yumi-san was also confronted with the distressing revelation: He has a mistress and has been financially supporting her for a very long time. This revelation of stress and guilt left her contemplating whether she should continue taking care of her parents. The overwhelming emotions made her contemplate fleeing from the situation altogether.

In addition to her caregiving responsibilities, Yumi-san holds a full-time job. This, all the while preparing meals for her family and attending to the daily needs of her parents before heading to work. She also manages their medical appointments. This puts her under constant pressure, resulting in the accumulation of stress and burnout, which takes a toll on her physical and emotional well-being. As time and energy devoted to caring for her parents and husband leave little room for social activities or nurturing personal relationships, she finds herself detached from friends and family, unable to engage in social events and to pursue her hobbies and interests

Recognizing the effects of neglecting the need for her own well-being, Yumi-san has discovered small things that brings her joy. She has understood the significance of self-care, and has thus compiled a list of simple pleasures to indulge in: whether it be visiting a cozy coffee shop, watching a movie, taking strolls at a particular place, listening to music, watching sunrise, sunset, buying flowers for herself, writing a letter to someone, taking a bubble bath, or talking to an old friend, and so on.

She also understands that her parent's wish is to remain in the comfort of their own home, rather than relocate to a care facility. So, whenever she finds herself on the verge of giving up, she reminisces about the love and support her parents gave her throughout her life.

Though life is far from easy, Yumi-san's deliberate acts of self-care, serves as a lifeline, allowing her to take care of her own well-being and the determination to do what is right to move forward.

Short Story

Building Happier Workplaces

Meet Natsu-san.

With close to a decade of experience as a human resource (HR) professional in the corporate sector, she has become acutely aware of the challenges posed by workplace stress. She has noticed, in particular, a recurring pattern of demotivation experienced by newly hired employees within months, who had showed enthusiasm with shining eyes on the first day. This observation fuelled her determination to address this issue and create a more sustainable, positive work environment for all employees.

The matter has troubled her to such an extent that she decided to study psychology. Presently, she is pursuing her master's degree at a university in Tokyo. Her ultimate goal is to aid companies in preventing new talent from experiencing demotivation in their professional environments.

Our team at Ikigai365 felt amazed after our interaction with Natsu-san. The dedication with which she strives to improve the workplace and make it a better environment is truly went beyond our imagination.

Currently, she is focusing her studies on *pawa hara*, a term used in Japan to describe workplace harassment where individuals misuse their authority or power to intimidate, belittle, or discriminate against subordinates or colleagues. This issue is prevalent among both men and women in Japan.

This term was coined by social psychologist and entrepreneur Okada Yasuko in 2003. Signifying power harassment, it is an outcome of recent changes in Japanese work culture that have led to an increase in workplace harassment, driven by a traditional hierarchical structure. This includes abusive, discriminatory, and exploitative behaviour from superiors towards employees due to a culture of micro-management and strict compliance norms.

In response to global developments in human rights and increased reporting of power harassment in court, in April 2020, Japan passed the Power Harassment Prevention Act. This law mandates companies to establish measures to prevent workplace bullying and implement an internal consultation process.

Power harassment can manifest in various forms, including excessive working hours, verbal abuse, information withholding, unfair treatment, undue pressure, and retaliation against those who speak up—to name a few.

As an HR counsellor, Natsu-san has been actively engaging with both the harassers and the harassed. Surprisingly, through her observations she has discovered that both parties often carry deep traumas. Surprisingly, even the harassers themselves experience anxiety, stress, and trauma, which they unconsciously pass on to those they target. In essence, a vicious cycle of mutual trauma is inflicted upon each other.

One of Natsu-san's life aspirations is to become a certified clinical psychologist. When asked about her plans after completing her degree, a spark of enthusiasm lights up her eyes, and she confidently responds, 'I will collaborate with senior leaders in workplaces to create a happier and safer environment.'

We further ask her if she sees a connection between Ikigai and her study of psychology. With a smile on her face, she replies, 'Perhaps I can assist someone in discovering their Ikigai. People should not merely work for financial reasons; they should work for a purpose that aligns with their life's calling, their Ikigai. I am determined to support them in this journey.'

Surprised by Natsu-san's remarkable clarity of purpose, we couldn't help but wonder what keeps her so motivated to pursue everything she is doing. Her response is truly inspiring.

Her home lies in Seisho coast, an area located in south-west of Kanagawa prefecture, approximately 70 kilometres away from Yokohama, where she stays for her studies. She follows a dedicated routine, staying in Yokohama from Monday to Friday each week. After a week's hard work, she returns to Seisho coast to spend weekends with her husband.

When we asked Natsu-san about what brings her the most amount of happiness and fulfilment, she revealed that she finds joy in both staying in and studying with young students in Tokyo and Yokohama during the week and going back to her hometown in Seisho coast on the weekends to her family. She admits that she cannot choose between the two, as each holds a special place in her heart. During her time in Yokohama, she cherishes the opportunity to be surrounded by fellow students, as she learns and grows together with them. On the other hand, her weekends spent in Seisho coast with her husband recharges her, preparing her for the upcoming week away from home.

Both aspects of her life, the academic pursuit in Tokyo/ Yokohama, and the family connection in Seisho coast, play a crucial role in making her life meaningful and satisfying.

When asked about how the course is helping her cope with her own anxiety and stress, Natsu-san's response is filled with inspiration and enthusiasm. She expresses that the course has been incredibly beneficial for her well-being. Each day, she feels genuinely inspired and eagerly looks forward to learning. Engaging in the study of psychology and understanding human behaviour has allowed her to gain valuable insights and tools to manage her own anxiety and stress.

The 2011 earthquake in Japan was another catalyst for Natsu-san's desire to learn psychology. This life-altering event prompted her to reflect on various aspects of her life, including her family, work, co-workers, and society as a whole. Witnessing the impact of such a significant natural disaster sparked a realization that she wanted to contribute something meaningful to those around her.

Natsu-san has turned her empathy and compassion into a meaningful mission. She is working hard to make workplaces happier and safer, aiming to bring positive changes to the lives of those she meets.

Ikigai365 Reflections > Action Tool

(This exercise takes approximately 60 minutes or longer to complete)
(Recommended frequency: Anytime you feel the need to step back/reflect/get a boost)

Here and Now
Present feelings or emotions
you are experiencing

Past memories
or experiences
triggered

Future
hopes or dreams
rekindled

What change
do you
choose to make

Now, what is the one action you will take today or start tomorrow ?

I will

Chapter 2 – Summer

Summer is marked by intense sunshine, high temperatures, and humidity with *furins* (wind chimes) offering comfort and signalling a refreshing breeze. This is also a time for colourful summer festivals and bright *hanabi* (Japanese fireworks) that bring people outside to celebrate.

The stories in this chapter reflect on people in their fifties and sixties who, despite facing the heat of responsibilities and challenges, find fulfilment in serving others by transforming the heat into light, bringing warmth and brightness into others' lives.

Caring is the Ultimate Form of Giving

Introducing Kato-san.

Life's secret mantra: (Inspired by/adapted from John Ruskin) 'Education is not about teaching people what they do not know, rather it is the challenge of continuously opening up the paths for them and leading by example.'

Caring for our own aging parents is something we all know we should do, but how many of us would actually step up to help others' elderly parents, especially if they're suffering from dementia? It's a challenging scenario that requires immense compassion and dedication.

At his elderly care centre, Change Evangelist, Kato-san not only dared to think differently about elderly care but also reimagined and redesigned aged care in Japan. His innovative approach focuses on creating an inclusive, intergenerational environment that benefits everyone involved.

In the summer of 2023, Ikigai365 team visited Aoi Care, an organization in Fujisawa that is 50 kilometres southwest of Tokyo and specializes in caring for older adults with dementia. As we arrived, we were greeted by the sight of beautiful flowers lining the path, leading to the centre. Inside, we saw elderly individuals, some in wheelchairs and others on foot, being assisted by both older and younger volunteers. They were preparing for an activity, and our curiosity led us to enquire further.

Kato-san explained that they were getting ready to go to the nearby park for *taiso*, a Japanese exercise routine that is part of their daily schedule. Taiso is known for benefiting people of all ages and abilities by promoting physical and mental well-being.

As we followed them to the park, the lively sounds of laughter and chatter filled the air. Upon arriving, we witnessed something remarkable: The park was thoughtfully divided into three sections—one for the elderly practicing taiso with slow, deliberate movements; another for kindergarten children cheerfully playing on swings; a third for seniors enjoying a round of gateball with their coach. The vibrant atmosphere brought together generations in a beautiful harmony.

Seeing everyone together was truly heart-warming. The intergenerational interaction was not only beneficial for the elderly, but also the children. It fostered a sense of community and mutual respect.

This experience at Aoi Care illustrates how rethinking elderly care can lead to innovative solutions that enhance the quality of life for all generations involved. Kato-san's vision of a community where everyone, regardless of age, can contribute and thrive is truly inspiring and sets a new standard for elderly care worldwide.

Now, you might be wondering why he started Aoi Care.

Let's explore further.

Kato-san comes from a family of educators who have been running a school since ages. Intending to continue his family's legacy, he pursued a bachelor's degree in education. However, circumstances changed when his uncle took over the family school, leaving Kato-san jobless after completing his studies. It was then that he decided to register with a recruitment agency, but the only position they offered was that of a caregiver. Thinking it would be temporary, he accepted the role, considering continuing to look for a more suitable job.

While working at this traditional elder care home, Kato-san closely observed how the residents were treated. A strict and rigid routine was imposed on them, dictating when they should eat, drink, sleep, or sit—regardless of their personal preferences or feelings at the time. Among many such experiences, one incident deeply impacted him and became a turning point in his life.

One day, a dementia patient expressed a heartfelt desire to see the *sakura*—the cherry blossom—and Kato-san wanted to fulfil the desire of that patient. But to his surprise, his request was rejected by the higher officials of the elder care home, who said that these patients can't go out of the vicinity and have to remain in the close boundary of the centre. They also said granting one wish would inevitably lead to an influx of more requests.

How could arbitrary rules deny these individuals such simple pleasures? They have lived their lives on their terms and may not be alive to see the sakura next year. Such questions made him leave his job and, at the age of twenty-five, he decided to obtain a loan to establish his own caregiving facility, where people with dementia could live on their own terms as other human beings. Driven by his personal experiences with bullying and loneliness as a youth, he understood the profound impact of finding a place where one truly belongs.

And now, Kato-san is questioning the usual rules followed at dementia care centres.

Typically, dementia care facilities are gated or locked to prevent residents from going out. However, the first thing he did was break the compound, opening it up so children could pass through on their way to school. In addition to this, Aoi Care is intentionally designed to be inclusive, featuring a cafeteria where locals gather for meals and study areas for children. Older adults mingle with care professionals and children daily, participating in all the daily talks of a meaningful life in the community.

Conventional care facilities maintain patient logs that track basic parameters, like whether they ate, slept, or took a shower. However, at Aoi Care, the logs focus on a different approach, recording how the patients felt, including their interactions and emotions. So, a lot of emphasis is given on the mental health of the patients.

In most centres, patients often just sit around doing nothing, and outsiders are brought in to entertain them. It's usually about others doing things for the patients—like giving them food or taking them outside. But at Aoi Care, Kato-san has created a place where everyone helps and supports each other. Even the elderly look out for one another. He believes dementia patients should get opportunities to show their skills and feel useful.

At Kato's care home, there is no rigid routine imposed on the residents. Instead, they are allowed to wake up at their leisure, eat meals based on their dietary needs, and sleep when they felt inclined. His philosophy extended beyond mere physical comfort: Kato-san recognized the importance of nurturing emotional well-being. He believes that the care has to be felt, and not told, because they may forget the words, but not how good they felt.

Many people believe that dementia is a disease, but Kato-san sees it as a syndrome. He explains that this condition comes with various symptoms, such as forgetfulness, memory loss, and reduced efficiency, but it is not an illness in itself. It is just like another syndrome.

Aoi Care stands out for its emphasis on strengthening relationships across generations and connecting with the community. It offers two primary services: residential housing for older adults dealing with dementia, and open day care centres accessible to the entire community, where older adults can visit and stay for a short period if they want to.

When a new patient joins the day care, Kato-san talks to their family to learn about the patient's interests, the kind of life they've lived, what have they gone through, and their emotions. The goal isn't to change their life, but to help them continue doing what they have been already doing. Many people are reluctant to come to day cares because they feel uncomfortable to be there. To help, Kato-san looks for ways to involve them in the centre's daily activities. This creates an environment where they feel comfortable and useful.

In fact, when we interacted with the volunteers and staff working at the centre, they all looked so happy, as if they felt alive and fulfilled each and every second spent there. It seemed that they didn't look at their work as just another ordinary job that they do for money, but as something that feeds their soul too.

Kato-san believes that caregivers don't choose this job for money. If money was their goal, they would pick other jobs. Caregivers work here because they truly want to help elderly people. At Aoi Care, many caregivers have young children and other responsibilities. Since the centre feels like a family, they bring their kids to work. Other caregivers and even the elderly patients help look after the children. It's like one big family supporting each other.

One of Kato-san's goals is to have more and more people understand dementia better, as it might be something natural that anybody could face in their later life. Drawing on the concept of muscle memory, he encourages residents to engage in familiar activities such as gardening, cooking, and various tasks that tap into their ingrained skills. Through these endeavours, he seeks to make them feel needed, valued, and useful. It is through the residents' own experiences of contributing and being part of a community that Kato-san aims to deliver a profound sense of care that transcends the limitations of memory.

In fact, when we were there, one of the ladies, skilled at making pickles brought them out and invited us to try. Others also displayed their creations, and we were all amazed by how beautifully they had crafted such delicate items. The moment felt so joyful that we spontaneously began dancing. Some of them sat and enjoyed the moment, while a few others couldn't resist and joined in, dancing along with us.

Additionally, Kato-san organizes local markets where the residents can sell their handmade crafts, pickles, and other products. These interactions foster a sense of happiness and fulfilment for the elders, while also challenging societal perceptions about dementia.

News of Kato's innovative approach to dementia care quickly spread far and wide. His work earned him recognition and accolades in numerous countries.

Kato-san says, 'The care should be given to the elders in the way they want to receive it, and not the way the caregiver wants to give.'

In the end, his story shows us how caring for elders can be about more than just following rules. It's about listening to what they need and want and treating them with dignity and kindness. By starting Aoi Care, he has changed how we think about looking after older people with dementia. His example teaches us that true care means making people feel valued and happy, even when they face challenges like memory loss.

Furthermore, Kato's holistic approach not only addresses the physical and mental well-being of the elderly but also enriches the community as a whole. By integrating activities that involve all generations, he strengthens a culture of empathy and mutual respect, bridging the gap between young and old. This interconnectedness creates a support network that benefits everyone, making Aoi Care a model for communities worldwide.

Prof. Hasegawa's Ikigai Expert Commentary

Kato-san has experienced many frustrating times and episodes through his adult life, but has consistently tried to create an environment he feels comfortable with and address the process of aging with dignity—something that we will all face in our lives ahead.

He is trying to change the traditional way of caring for elders and seniors, prioritizing making everyone involved feel comfortable, both physically and emotionally. This is his unique approach to valuing the present in a way that it values the future better than the past. With his efforts, he finds fulfilment and satisfaction by creating a caring environment for both elders and his staff. Thus, he channels his anger and frustration at the status-quo, along with his past experiences into feeling both alive and fulfilled.

Self-determination theory (SDT) is a psychological framework that studies how people develop and are motivated, as well as how social and cultural factors can impact their well-being.[12]

It proposes that people have three fundamental psychological needs that are essential for humans to flourish: Autonomy (feeling in control of one's own life and choices), Competence (feeling capable and effective in one's actions), Relatedness (feeling connected to and cared for by others). SDT examines various types of motivation as well as the impact of social context and has been applied in a wide range of domains including education, work, parenting, healthcare, and psychotherapy.

The 'agent' as key to self-determination fits well with the Three Elements of Ikigai model, where self is the agent of change. In Kato-san's story, he not only uses self-determination to design a new model of senior care, but he is also creating conditions for the seniors at Aoi Care to be their own agents, so that they feel in control, capable, and connected. This would lead to supporting each senior's Ikigai while they are there.

Your present self is your biggest tool or weapon in your own life and Ikigai journey. It is your agent of feeling the emotions in the here-and-now and linking these to the various triggers and experiences.

Although its origin is unclear, there is a Japanese proverb that goes like, 'Don't scold children; it is the road you have come from. Don't laugh at old people; it is the road you are heading to.' The road you have come from, and the road you are going to, is a two-person journey. The road you will take today you cannot redo; it is the road that will take you to the future. This two-person journey described here refers not to a specific person, but rather to the feelings that accompany the journey of life. It is similar to one's Ikigai that accompanies one's life journey.

Heartfelt advice for you from Kato-san

I believe that care should be given to elders in the way they want to receive it and not the way that we think is best for them.

We hope Kato-san's story resonated with you and stirred something within. Let us gently invite you to take a small step forward on your own Ikigai365 journey.

Close your eyes and take a deep breath, reflecting on the following questions before writing down the answers:

When you were younger, what were some of your dreams?

_____

_____

_____

Is there a current dream you are not pursuing, which you might regret later on?

_____

If Kato-san can, so can you. Take that first step today!

Sidebar: Dementia Care in Japan

According to a study by the Ministry of Health, Labor, and Welfare in Tokyo, it is estimated that by 2060, one in six elderly individuals in Japan, or about 17.7 per cent of those aged sixty-five and older, will likely have dementia. Additionally, another 6.32 million elderly people, or 17.4 percent of those sixty-five and older, are expected to have mild cognitive impairment, a stage prior to dementia.[13]

Addressing this issue is crucial. One promising approach involves utilizing muscle memory in dementia patients, which can help improve their well-being. Muscle memory refers to the body's ability to perform tasks without conscious thought, typically developed through repetition over time. By focusing on muscle memory, caregivers can create opportunities for dementia patients to experience moments of joy, satisfaction, and connection to their past selves, ultimately enhancing their quality of life.

Numerous research studies and documents discuss the positive impact of leveraging muscle memory and familiar activities for dementia patients.[14]

By incorporating these strategies, we can make a meaningful difference in the lives of those affected by dementia, promoting a sense of dignity and purpose.

Key quote

'People will never remember what you said or what you did, but they'll never forget how you made them feel'.

—Carl W. Buehner

Smile of Gratitude Lights
up the Heart

Walk with Midori-san.

Life's secret mantra: 'Life is short, so I choose to count my blessings and not my sufferings.'

Midori-san was born into a family where her mother fell ill shortly after her birth. Consequently, she doesn't have many memories of her mother being well or performing normal household chores. During her early years, she was primarily raised by her father, with support from their neighbours. From a young age, Midori-san helped care for her mother, who required regular visits from nurses. Witnessing the kindness and assistance provided by them inspired Midori-san to become a nurse herself.

As she grew older, Midori-san pursued her dream and successfully became a nurse. At twenty-five, she got married and had a son. Unfortunately, her marriage quickly turned abusive, with her husband resorting to domestic violence. The situation worsened over time, as he even began inflicting violence on their son. Realizing that she and her child were in danger, Midori-san made the difficult decision to divorce her husband. However, he did not accept the divorce and responded with increased violence, while refusing to provide any financial support. But despite the emotional abuse and financial hardships, Midori-san persevered. She remained determined to provide her son with a good education and a safe, nurturing environment. To secure a house, she took out a loan and purchased a small apartment.

The divorce process, combined with the lack of financial and emotional support, took a toll on Midori-san's mental health. She fell into severe depression, struggling to find the motivation to work or engage in daily activities. The love for her son compelled her to keep pushing forward. She realized that the child had no one else to rely on but her, and that thought became her driving force to overcome the depression and care for her son's needs.

Also, working as a nurse in various departments, including the children's general ward, over multiple home visits, she saw the pain and suffering of the parents more than the children. She was grateful to come home to a healthy child, which was enough for her. Seeing him smile lifted her mood and brought a smile to her own face as well. Slowly, she realized that seeing others smile makes her happy. This is when she started helping others. When nothing else was in her control, this was: doing something for someone else. Someone saying thank you to her, and her reciprocating it to someone else, was a ray of hope. She felt she wasn't alone.

Even though Midori-san's life is difficult, she managed to maintain a positive attitude and a deep sense of gratitude. Despite limited financial resources, she found joy in small things and constantly changed the decoration of their home with inexpensive items. This uplifted her mood and created a sense of freshness. She calls it *chichai tanoshimi*, which means small happiness.

She uses everyday objects to give a seasonal feeling, only by changing a few things around. She puts up happy pictures of her friends as well as of herself with her son all around, and seeing them makes her even happier, reminding her that she's blessed.

For example, if she buys a hat, she will put it along with the other decorations and admire it. If someone gives her some cookies or a piece of cake, she will display it on a nice plate before eating it, appreciating it with gratitude. Just listening to music, going for a walk, appreciating the flowers and trees along the way, and meeting a friend or someone for a conversation—all these bring her joy. When alone, she is consumed by her thoughts and misery, so even simple acts like going to a restaurant, enjoying a meal, and thanking the owner make her happy.

When there's darkness in your heart, it's like opening up a little window to let the brightness enter.

To find happiness and joy in small everyday things, she nurtured a skill of amplifying joy and gratitude. She believes that one can train themselves to feel more. 'If your level of joy and gratitude for a thing is at one, try to amplify it to two, and slowly to three, and so on,' she says. 'Until you reach the level of ten and your heart is full of love, gratitude, and joy.'

This has become her way of life and second nature. She advises not to wait for big things in life to experience joy, because they are far less frequent.

She has a liking for things from the UK and always dreamed of taking her son there. Over time, she saved up enough money and, when her son was ten, she took him to London for a week. That trip was her way of showing her son that they were okay and that she was back in control of her life. It was the first and last trip they went on outside of Japan. She has pictures of this trip decorated all around her house, serving as a constant reminder that she can overcome difficulties and relive the happy moments of their trip.

However, life had more challenges in store for Midori-san. She was diagnosed with spastic paraplegia, an autoimmune disease that affects her muscle control. The prognosis was disheartening, as it meant she would progressively lose the ability to walk and eventually lose control of her hands.

'As men, we are all equal in the presence of death,' the quote by Publilius Syrus, had a great influence on Midori-san. It made her realize that death is the great equalizer. No matter what happens during our time on earth, death will eventually overtake us all.

So, instead of comparing herself with others who have more money, better family, and health, she decided to focus on the commonality we all share—death. She thought of living her life on her own terms and do whatever she could for others and herself.

'I may not have the wealth or health others do, but I'm going to die like those who have it. So, why not do everything in my power until my death? Why not live a life worthy of myself?' she says. '*Jibunrashiku*' which is Japanese for 'in your own way' or 'true to yourself.'

Instead of focusing on what's lost, Midori-san chooses to focus on what remains in her life. When asked if she ever had a moment of 'Why me?', she agrees.

'But soon, I realized it cannot be treated with current medicine. With half a feeling of despair and the other half a small ray of hope, I look forward to small things, doing what's in my control, reducing expectations, and valuing things around me and every interaction with others. I programmed myself not to dwell on things that cannot be changed.'

And now, she believes in reducing expectations. The world and people don't owe her anything, and how she lives the rest of her life is her choice. She can keep questioning why it happened to her, and blame others for her circumstances, but that won't change anything. She may not have the health and wealth of others, but she has a son and can smile while making others do the same, and that's good enough for her, she says.

Despite the devastating news, Midori-san refuses to give up. She finds gratitude in every challenge she faces. For example, she sees the fifteen steps leading to her apartment as a metaphor for the life she desires—each step is a step forward to a life filled with love, happiness, and her beloved son waiting for her. This makes her happy to climb the stairs, instead of seeing them as a hurdle.

Currently, Midori-san is focusing on making her home accessible for her impending physical limitations. She understands that her mobility will decrease over time and doesn't want to burden her son with the task of rearranging the house later. Additionally, she continues to work in a desk job, doing patient care paperwork. Soon, she will not be able to use her hands and legs, and maybe other parts of her body. Now, she's preparing herself to look for a caregiving job that only involves talking within her abilities. She wants to continue caring for people while she still can, believing that helping others will uplift her. Her son, inspired by her resilience, has chosen a career path as a physiotherapist and caregiver to help others.

During recent tests, the doctor informed her that her condition was worsening faster than expected, and that she needed to prepare herself for becoming totally immobile. This news got her down, and she was upset for a whole day. But she gathered herself with her usual ways of trying to be helpful to someone and promising herself to focus on what she is grateful for.

When asked about her Ikigai, she says for someone like her, who is facing deteriorating health, it's hard to look forward to anything., The word Ikigai, then, is a bit heavy. This is why she has decided not to think about living for a particular purpose and, instead, focus on small happiness and *yorokobi*—or joy—on what's available at that moment and on that day, like looking forward to talking to someone or smiling at something. She also believes in reliving good memories and creating new ones with small things is important.

Her advice to someone feeling lonely, despaired, and depressed is not to lie down and stare at the ceiling. It's the same thing she had advised her patients as a nurse. 'If you cannot go out, at least open the curtains and look outside. Moving clouds, people walking, and swinging leaves help you see that there's movement in life,' she says. 'Also, remember that you're not alone. Among the eight billion people in the world, is it really true that there's no one to talk to or who can understand and relate to you? It's just us isolating ourselves in our own thoughts. Don't try too hard; you're good enough as you are and have faith that someone will help you in some way.'

She continues. 'Also, believe in a tomorrow and that it will be better. Finally, remember that there's always someone else who has it worse than you, who would gladly trade places with you. None of us are ever truly alone. In life's hardest moments, someone will always be there to support and lift you up.'

This perspective can help us feel things are almost never as bad as they seem. So, with that faith, let's greet today with gratitude and a heartfelt smile and a simple 'thank you'.

Prof. Hasegawa's Ikigai Expert Commentary

When I read Midori-san's story, I found myself reflecting again on the real essence of Ikigai. I was reminded of what I consistently observed over the last decades: It is about discovering small joys in the surroundings in which I live. Ikigai is usually translated into English as 'the purpose of life', or its meaning. A person's life itself has two meanings: a period of time—the daily life, for instance—and the whole lifetime itself.

When I developed the Three Elements of Ikigai, I tried to create its practical concept, focusing on time and consciousness. The perception of time has aspects of a psychological phenomenon that can be subjectively lengthened or shortened. Whenever I experience falling down on a snowy road, where my feet slip and I lose my balance, the time until my body hit the ground proceeded slowly—as if in slow motion. I interpret this as an experience of an altered state of consciousness in self-protection, to delay the pain as much as possible. This is consistent with my experience from seminars where people who fall down from the top of stairs have experienced a similar sense of slowing time!

Such experiences are the common everyday trance, where altered states of consciousness (ASC) occur spontaneously.[15]

And the use of ASC in psychotherapy is the foundation of hypnotherapy. The ASC is also related to hypnosis, which is, in fact, also defined as an ASC elicit through human communication.

Midori-san has episodes of such increasing or decreasing subjective experiences in daily life. I believe her experience is the common everyday trance in daily living.

Viktor Frankl (1905–1997), the author of *Man's Search For Meaning*, advocates three value categories in his book. Creative values (*schöpferische werte*) are values that create something new in the world by human action of creation. Experiential values (*erlebnis werte*) are values that one receives from the world and experiences that move one's heart, such as when exposed to art or nature. Attitudinal values (*einstellungs werte*) are created by how we perceive meaning in even the toughest situations, and by what attitude we adopt and how we behave. Attitudinal values is the value of a more humane attitude, a value that no one can take away.

Midori-san's work as a nurse or engaged in child-care engaged her with creative values. She also engaged with experiential values when redecorating her room. She is characterized mainly by attitudinal values, and it can be said that she has survived in the face of adversity in the eyes of others. Her early childhood, seeing an unwell mother who couldn't perform even basic household chores, being supported by neighbours and regular visits from nurses instilled a kindness that she then practiced as nursing care in her adult work. Midori-san also has a deep sense of gratitude for others and a humane sense of existence, no matter how harsh the surrounding reality and future outlook.

Like Midori-san, try to tune into your 'attitudinal values' and focus your Ikigai journey on (a) what motivates you to live from your memories of the past, (b) what motivates you to live in the present here-and-now, and (c) what motivates you to live in the future by imagining it in the present.

These continuous back-and-forth between the past, present, and future are fundamental realities to your Ikigai journey.

> **Heartfelt advice for you from Midori-san**
>
> Bring a smile to someone and light up their world with a small act of kindness and gratitude. That smile then reflects back, filling your own heart with happiness. As this cycle repeats, the small flame of kindness grows brighter, illuminating even the most difficult paths in life.

We hope Midori-san's story stirred something powerful inside you!

Let's turn that feeling into action—your Ikigai365 journey is ready to begin.

> **Close your eyes and take a deep breath, reflecting on the following questions before writing down the answers:**
>
> Think about something in your life that you keep complaining about and have been bothered by for some time.
>
> _____
>
> _____
>
> _____
>
> And then, zoom out and observe all the different people and things you are grateful for.
>
> _____

If Midori-san can, so can you. Take that first step today!

Sidebar: Naikan Therapy: The Art of Self-Reflection

Naikan therapy is a Japanese introspective practice designed to help individuals reflect on their lives and relationships. The term *naikan* translates to 'looking inside' or 'introspection'.

This form of therapy was developed in the 1940s by Yoshimoto Ishin, a Buddhist practitioner, and is based on Buddhist principles, particularly the teachings on gratitude and interconnectedness.

There are three fundamental questions that one asks oneself:

- What have I received from that person (a particular person one may think of)?
- What have I given to that person?
- What troubles and difficulties have I caused to that person?

The goal of a typical naikan practice is to gain insight into one's own thoughts and actions, while cultivating a sense of gratitude and interdependence. By deeply examining the ways we interact with and impact others, we can cultivate a more compassionate and fulfilling life.

Whether practiced in intensive retreats or guided sessions, naikan therapy provides valuable insights that can lead to personal growth and healing.

Key quote

'You only live once? False. You live every day. You only die once.'

—Anonymous

'Creating My Own *Ibasho* - A Place to Belong'

Meet Hanazawa-san.

Life's secret mantra: '*Kekka orai*. All's well that ends well.'

Hanazawa-san's journey began at her parents' restaurant, where she helped out as a young girl. At eighteen, she started working part-time at a local warehouse, where she met her husband. They got married soon after and had three children, who are now aged thirty, twenty-eight, and eighteen respectively. Raising her kids kept Hanazawa-san extremely busy, and without a formal degree, working in an office wasn't an option. Her social interactions were mostly limited to other young mothers, and their conversations revolved around children and family life.

Though she cherished these moments, and her life as a full-time mom had been fulfilling, she yearned for something more. She wanted to learn more about society and interact with people from different age groups and backgrounds, hear their experiences, and broaden her understanding of the society. That's when she had an idea that would change her life and those around her.

She was part of a *mamatomo* group. Made up of two words, *mama* meaning 'mom', and *tomo*, meaning 'friend', the term refers to the friendships formed between mothers of children who are friends—often through school, daycare, or neighbourhood activities. One day, Hanazawa-san realized that one of the moms was really good at making *ikebana*, the traditional Japanese art of flower arrangement. 'You're so talented at this! Why don't you teach all of us?' she said. 'I can host the classes at my place, and you can teach us there.'

She then approached various other mamatomos, and that's how it all began.

The first class had just three people, but from there, everything took off.

By inviting people to her house, she could learn new things while providing a space for others to do the same. She believed many women like her also sought company and opportunities to learn. Hanazawa-san wanted to create a welcoming space, where everyone felt they belonged and could enjoy each other's company.

Soon, her house became a bustling hub for women in the neighbourhood and beyond to meet, learn, share knowledge, and support one another. Over next ten years, she hosted these activities and made countless friends and formed deep, meaningful connections.

Hanazawa-san's gatherings were unlike any typical meetups. While most people gather at a friend's house for casual conversations, her gatherings had a completely different energy: The moment you entered her home, you couldn't help but amaze at how everyone was immersed in something they loved or were skilled at.

Someone might be arranging flowers beautifully, another tuning a guitar—each person fully engaged in their own passion. Yet, there was a collective spirit that brought everyone together; it didn't feel like a class or a standard social event. In contrast to the usual Japanese setting, where people often wait for instructions or direction, everyone here participated out of their own free will. It was the kind of environment that naturally drew people in and made them want to be part of it.

Hanazawa-san thrived on these interactions, which kept her busy and fulfilled. However, hosting a large group had its challenges. At one gathering, twenty-five people signed up for a lesson, and she was stressed about buying and storing the ingredients needed to feed everyone. In her search for recipes that could be prepared ahead of time and didn't require refrigeration, she stumbled upon one for fermented food. The dish was a hit, sparking her interest in learning more about fermentation.

Unfortunately, soon after, Covid-19 forced her to shut down her activities. During the pandemic, Hanazawa-san faced several challenges. She missed meeting new people and sharing experiences. Additionally, she struggled with her health, particularly her gut health, as the restrictions made it difficult to access fresh fruits and vegetables. Whenever she had access to buy them, she wanted it to last longer too. Thus continued her research on preserving fresh fruits and vegetables by fermenting, even deciding to experiment more with them.

As Hanazawa-san experimented with fermented food, she noticed something remarkable: the quality and taste of the food varied depending on her mood and overall well-being. Whenever she was in a bad mood, the food spoiled quickly; but when she was in a good mood, the fermentation process resulted in better-tasting and longer-lasting food. This revelation had a profound impact on her, emphasizing the connection between her emotions and the food she prepared. She also noticed a significant improvement in her own health and energy levels. Her gut issues were resolved, and she felt better overall.

Once Covid-19 restrictions eased, Hanazawa-san was eager to share her newfound knowledge. She resumed her activities and started teaching others to cook with fermented food. As she shared her expertise, people loved her recipes and started seeing improvements in their own health too.

This motivated her to reach out to more people and share the benefits she'd learned about, which led her to combine her love for music and fermented food.

Hanazawa-san was a fan of music festivals, where food trucks typically sold fast food like fries, fried chicken, and hot dogs.

She thought, 'Why not offer healthy, fermented food options instead?' Encouraged by her husband, she bought a food truck and transformed it to have a rusted exterior, naming it Ferrum. She believed the rustic look symbolized old roots and natural eating.

But to legally run the food truck, she needed a commercial kitchen, so she opened a small restaurant and named it Wabi Sabi, where she served dishes made only with fermented food. When she started it, all her friends came together to support her, even helping with the painting. The plates in her restaurant were specially crafted by one such who did the pottery work just for her. She continues to run classes there, teaching fermented food recipes and their benefits.

The name 'Wabi Sabi', a Japanese aesthetic that finds beauty in imperfection and transience, was deeply meaningful to Hanazawa-san. It embraces the idea that life can leave its mark, and beauty doesn't need to be perfect, valuing the rustic, the weathered, and the imperfect. Hanazawa-san sees beauty in rusted old things. She believes that just as rust adds character to old objects, imperfections can add beauty and depth to our lives. She wanted her restaurant to embody this philosophy.

Hanazawa-san's experience as a teenage mother allowed her to empathize with the struggles faced by younger moms. Because she understands the challenges of raising children, providing nutritious meals, and managing mental health, through her teachings, she teaches young mothers how their energy, mood, and stress affect the fermentation process. By demonstrating how emotions impact food quality, she encouraged them to find healthier ways to handle stress and improve their well-being.

One such example was when a staff member at her restaurant struggled with fermenting vegetables. The more the staff member worried about the outcome, the worse the fermentation process became. Hanazawa-san advised her to stay calm and not to be anxious over the results, reassuring her that if the vegetables were over-fermented, they could be used for something else, like salad dressing. After adopting this mindset, the staff member noticed better results. Hanazawa-san continues to observe how emotions affect food and applies the same concept to life, realizing *nantoka naru* (somehow things will work out) serves her best.

By hosting regular markets and gatherings at her restaurant, Hanazawa-san continues to support women who need a platform to showcase their talent and sell their creations. She wanted to create an *ibasho*, a place where women felt they belonged and were cared for, just as she longed for such a place herself. The women continue to gather there, help and encourage each other in their businesses and new ventures.

When asked about her progress from a housewife to a business owner, she smiles. 'Sometimes, it's better not to think too much and simply do what you want to do'.

Her heartfelt advice to other women?

Trust yourselves and act on your urges to try something new. She believes that doubts and second-guessing can hinder progress, but taking the first step makes the rest easier. Her secret mantra is *kekka orai*, which means 'if the result is okay, everything related to it is too'. All's well that ends well, in simpler terms.

Now, she focuses on the positive outcomes, even in negative situations, and looks for the good that can come from them.

Currently, Hanazawa-san enjoys taking her food truck to remote places, serving fermented food, connecting with locals, making new friends with the other food truck owners, and learning new things. Through these experiences, her ultimate vision is to spread awareness about the connection between positive feelings, fermented food, and overall well-being.

Prof. Hasegawa's Ikigai Expert Commentary

Exposure at an early age to familiar family activities is the beginning of contact with society. It is also not limited to domestic chores like cooking, cleaning, caring for, or being taken care of by a family member. If the family runs a farm or a business, it also adds to the experience of being connected to society by watching the family work and interacting with a variety of people who are related to the work—employees, customers, and partners, etc.

For example, I spent my childhood thinking that I would follow my grandfather and father's steps. My family ran an ironworks factory that manufactured parts for cars and machinery. I remember my grandfather, grandmother, father, and employees together operating the machines and process its parts, while my mother handled accounting and answered the phone. I also recall the smiling faces of the employees who talked to me, the sound of the machines, and the smell of oils in the factory.

The family is the gateway that connects us to society. Hanazawa-san grew up in one that owned a restaurant and was familiar with the idea of providing something for others. After having a child in her late-teenage and bringing up her children, she discovered the joy of opening up her home and providing an ibasho, or a place, where she could learn and interact with other mothers raising children, as well as serving the food she had grown accustomed to in her childhood.

The 'Need to Belong' hypothesis is a foundational theory in social psychology, arguing that the need to belong is a basic human motivation and essential for psychological and physical well-being.[16] This theory provides a framework for understanding why humans seek social connections, the consequences of lacking them, and the dynamics of forming and maintaining relationships.

The two key requirements that shape our sense of belonging are (a) frequent, positive interactions with other that are regular, meaningful, and free from hostility; and (b) stable, enduring relationships—a sense of mutual concern and care over long periods of time. This is deeply linked to our evolution as humans, because belonging to groups increased survival chances by providing protection, access to resources, and opportunities for reproduction.

Hanazawa-san's childhood dreams were shaped by her experiences at her family's restaurant. However, these were likely postponed or became out of reach once she became a teenage mother. Not wanting to wallow in self-pity nor give up on her dreams, her interactions with other young mothers gave her the spark to create a place where everyone felt safe, welcomed, and belonged. This resulted in a community where everyone found fulfilment in everyday life, as well as continuously renewed their motivation to live, learn, and thrive, despite multiple challenges.

For example, the fermented foods products that she worked on, was during the period when providing a physical place was suspended during Covid-19. Her food offerings reflected the results of research that Hanazawa-san focused on through her experiences in childcare and her own health status.

In the beginning, there may have been a feeling of emptiness inside. So, she may have brought objects from outside as they made her feel good. She also realized that the stage she created made others feel the same. This free flow of repeated interactions led to her discovering the kitchen car and restaurant, as she realized these made her feel alive and thus it became her Ikigai. She also continued to support bringing others together, as she realized that it makes them feel supported, belonged, satisfied which, in turn, made her feel fulfilled.

Heartfelt advice for you from Hanazawa-san

Your Ikigai may, in fact, be hidden nearby—right next to you. You may even have to take a courageous step to discover it. It is all up to you to listen to your inner voice to understand what *you* really want. Accordingly, take small steps in fulfilling your heart's desires.

We hope Hanazawa-san's story lit a little spark within you. Take this as a gentle encouragement to start shaping your own Ikigai365 story today.

Close your eyes and take a deep breath, reflecting on the following questions before writing down the answers:

Who did you help or care for in the past one week? How did you show that you care for them?

_____

_____

_____

Who helped or cared for you in the past one week? How did they show they care for you?

_____

_____

_____

You may wish to use the tool 'Lifeline Mapping' in myIkigai365 nourishment journal.

If Hanazawa-san, can, so can you! Take that first step today!

Sidebar: Moai and Yuimaru, the Japanese Support System

Moai means 'meeting for a common purpose'. It's a social support group built around shared interests or companionship, providing emotional, practical support, a sense of belonging, purpose, and connection.

Imagine having a small group of close friends who have your back no matter what: people who support you emotionally, financially, or in any way you need. That's what moai is all about. It's like a support squad where everyone chips in, shares the load, and celebrates life together. With modern life being so hectic and isolating, creating your own moai—even just a group of friends who meet regularly—can provide a sense of security and belonging.

Yuimaru refers to 'circle of connection'. It symbolizes reciprocity and interdependence, where everyone contributes for the common good, fostering gratitude and respect for shared resources.

It is more about the 'we' instead of just the 'me'—an idea that when we help each other, the whole community thrives. Think of it as neighbours pitching in during tough times or sharing responsibilities to make everyone's life easier. This mindset helps when facing big challenges, whether it's raising a family, dealing with a disaster, or simply creating a friendlier neighbourhood.

It's about recognizing that together, we're stronger.

Key quote

'Be yourself—everyone else is taken'.

—Oscar Wilde

Short Story

Balance Impact With Connection

Meet Sumida-san.

Yoshioki Sumida sounds like an extraordinary individual with a deep connection to his ancestral roots and traditional Japanese samurai culture. With over twenty years of experience in both swordsmanship and *yabusame* (archery on horseback), he has developed his skills to an exceptional degree.

His dedication to teaching genuine swordsmanship and sharing the authentic samurai spirit with foreign visitors is commendable. By doing so, he not only preserves and passes on the ancient traditions but also helps promote cross-cultural understanding and appreciation for Japan's rich historical heritage.

As a descendant of samurai, Sumida-san carries a unique responsibility to uphold and pass down the legacy of his ancestors. By dedicating his life to this mission, he is contributing to the preservation and appreciation of a culture that has shaped Japan's history and identity.

On a rainy day, we had the privilege of meeting the master at his *dojo*—a training hall for practicing martial arts—located in a quiet residential area. Despite our slight delay, the master had been eagerly waiting for our arrival, as he had an important meeting to attend later, and thus wanted to make the most of the available time for our training.

His restlessness and sense of urgency showcase his dedication to his craft and his commitment to ensuring that he provided us with a meaningful and impactful session. He understood the value of time and wanted to make every moment count in passing on the genuine spirit of the samurai to us.

As the training began, you could sense his passion and devotion to the twin arts of swordsmanship and yabusame. He carefully guided us through each movement, ensuring we understood the significance and philosophy behind every technique. His dedication to preserving the authenticity of the samurai tradition became evident as he emphasized the importance of adhering to the principles of bushido and incorporating them into the practice.[17]

Bushido, the code that set samurai apart in feudal Japan, finds its roots in the word *bushi*, meaning warrior. Samurai, often referred to as 'those who serve', embodied this code. Their lives, like sakura trees, were beautiful, glorious, but brief. Bushido consists of eight virtues: justice, courage, compassion, respect, integrity, honour, loyalty, and self-control.

Although initially designed for warriors, these principles can be adapted to modern life, fostering personal growth, discipline, and ethical behaviour. Integrating some or all of these principles can lead to a more virtuous and fulfilling life.

As we settled down, the master closed his fists and instructed us to push him. Surprisingly, we found it quite easy to push him back with force. However, he then relaxed his posture slightly and encouraged us to push him again. To our amazement, we were unable to move his hands even an inch.

The demonstration by the master emphasizes the importance of finding the right balance between firmness and relaxation in martial arts. When you overly tense your body and mind while being pushed, you focus your energy on resisting the force, causing you to lose your balance. Conversely, when you relax your body and mind and approach the attacker with the right frame of mind, your force increases and the opponent is unable to topple you over. By harmonizing with the incoming force and redirecting it, you gain stability and power, making your opponent's efforts ineffective.

The lesson from martial arts extends far beyond combat and applies to all aspects of life. The principle of approaching tasks with a relaxed and focused mindset, aiming to achieve a state of flow, is a powerful concept that can lead to greater success and fulfilment.

By adopting a relaxed approach and allowing oneself to be open and adaptable, you let go of your ego and become one with the universe, getting better at harnessing your skills and creativity. Instead of relying solely on brute force or intense effort, the individual can tap into the power of being in sync with the task at hand. This not only enhances performance but also reduces stress and enables a deeper connection with the task or activity.

It's fascinating to learn that in the early years of his career, Sumida-san worked at a trading company and had no interest in swords. However, fate had a unique plan for him. One fine day, he found himself assisting in a competition, helping with tasks like rolling and lifting mats. It was during this event that they were also selling swords.

As Sumida-san laid eyes on one of the swords, he asked the master if he could take it home. Upon bringing it back, he held it in his hand and felt it. It was at this moment he knew that he wanted to learn the art of swordsmanship.

Talking about how samurai are depicted in *chanbara* (samurai cinema), Sumida-san is not too happy. Indeed, many such movies are created with the primary goal of entertaining audiences, and as a result, they often take artistic liberties and exaggerate certain aspects of the samurai way of life.

Sumida-san's dedication to teaching authentic swordsmanship and sharing the genuine samurai spirit with foreign visitors is particularly important given the misunderstandings fuelled by popular culture. By sharing his authentic knowledge and insights, he can help correct misconceptions and promote a more accurate understanding of the rich legacy of the samurai in Japanese history.

As we bid goodbye to the master and exit the dojo, we take with us a fresh understanding and respect for the authentic essence of Japanese samurai culture. The encounter has left a lasting impact, and we feel inspired to continue our journey of learning and understanding the ways of the samurai.

Short Story

Strength + Beauty = Self-Worth

Meet Miho-san.

Miho-san grew up in a traditional Japanese setting with five siblings, but she always felt a desire to break free from societal norms and expectations. When she met her foreigner husband at a party, she instantly fell in love with him. Despite their cultural and religious differences (Miho-san being Buddhist, and her husband Christian), their mutual respect and admiration for each other's beliefs and values brought them together.

Miho-san's husband faced significant challenges, when he first arrived in Japan. As a foreigner entering Japanese society, he encountered resistance and struggled to establish himself. However, with perseverance and hard work, he eventually made a name for himself in the industry. Miho-san being a diligent and supportive partner, played a role in assisting him with his business, contributing to its growth and success.

However, as they started raising their children, cultural clashes and differing expectations became more pronounced. Miho-san's husband began imposing his own cultural values and standards on their children, often conflicting with the typical Japanese upbringing. This led to escalating tensions and blame being placed on Miho-san for not being good enough to her husband's expectations.

Feeling responsible and questioning her worth, she embarked on a journey of self-discovery and self-improvement. She turned to books and research, seeking answers to fix the problems in her marriage.

Fortunately, Miho-san confided in a sister at her church, who recognized the signs of emotional abuse and reassured her that she was not at fault. This realization was a turning point for Miho-san, as she understood the importance of working on herself first and establishirg boundaries in her marriage. Despite contemplating leaving, she chose to stay and put effort into transforming her relationship.

Gaining confidence and perspective, Miho-san started to communicate her needs and concerns to her husband more effectively. She also discovered the importance of how she conveyed her thoughts, realizing that good communication is not only about what is said but also how it is said. This change in approach helped foster understanding and growth within their marriage.

Throughout her journey, Miho-san faced the pressure of maintaining a perfect image to society, especially because she had married internationally. However, as she focused on her own well-being and prioritized self-care, she gradually let go of those expectations, embracing her true self and finding fulfilment in her own hobbies and interests.

Miho-san's experience with cancer further heightened her perspective on life and the importance of personal happiness. It helped her to prioritize her own needs and not lose herself in the pursuit of perfection.

Miho-san embodies beauty and strength like a bamboo tree—just like the folklore about the Chinese bamboo trees, which serves as a remarkable metaphor for resilience and delayed success. Despite no visible growth in the first five years, these trees shoot up ninety feet in just five weeks. This story underscores the importance of perseverance in achieving goals, urging us not to give up during initial setbacks in personal or professional life. Continuous nurturing is the key for long-term success.

Miho-san realized that instead of trying to focus on having a perfect marriage, becoming a perfect mom or wife, and trying to make her international marriage work and put pressure on herself, it is important for her to focus on her own self-care. Taking time out to do things that make her feel alive, meeting and socializing with her friends (which she had forgotten earlier because of being so busy with family, kids, husband) and above all taking care of her own physical and emotional well-being. Working on all this helped her gain more confidence, and this hereby improved her marriage, and she found greater happiness and fulfilment.

Her story underscores the significance of self-worth, setting boundaries, effective communication, and personal growth in overcoming cultural differences and emotional abuse within a marriage.

Today, Miho-san is proud of the way of life her husband has built and feels happy to be able to work with her son to carry on the family business and further its prosperity. She says that her most important Ikigai in life is to cherish the family ties and pass on the traditions of both her and the husband's families to the next generation.

Now that you have read all the stories in the Summer chapter, may we invite you to pause to complete the Ikigai365 Reflection > Action Tool below. It is our way to help you continue tuning-in to your own seeds of sources and feelings of Ikigai.

Ikigai365 Reflections > Action Tool

(This exercise takes approximately 60 minutes or longer to complete)
(Recommended frequency: Anytime you feel the need to step back/reflect/get a boost)

Here and Now
Present feelings or emotions
you are experiencing

Past memories
or experiences
triggered

Future
hopes or dreams
rekindled

What change
do you
choose to make

Now, what is the one action you will take today or start tomorrow ?

I will

Chapter 3 – Autumn

Autumn is a time to celebrate, reflect, and appreciate the beauty of nature. The maple leaves turn red and golden, and nature shows us how to accept change, while enjoying different kinds of food and sports that make the season even more special.

The stories in this chapter, featuring people in their seventies and eighties, are about living colourful, energetic lives and feeling alive. Each falling leaf is like letting go of something, while the bright colours remind us of happy memories and rich experiences.

Life Becomes Worthy When You Start 'Living It'

Step into Masako-san's world.

Life's secret mantra: *Yaro to omottara yareru*—where there is a will, there is always a way. Every day is a fresh opportunity to actively celebrate life with what I can do today and with what I have. Don't waste time and energy on complaints, regrets, or dwelling on the past and have an unconditional acceptance of the present.

Masako-san, at the age of eighty-three, runs Kaishinzan, a ramen restaurant in Meguro ward, Tokyo, all by herself, without any help. She, along with her late husband, has been in the restaurant business for the past fifty-five years.

Her husband was a cook at the Chinese embassy for many years, who then decided to open a restaurant of his own. Masako-san was a homemaker until then, and when her husband needed help, she decided to join him. However, her job at the restaurant was always in the kitchen, and her husband did not let her interact with the customers. He was very orthodox and regressive in his thinking, and she conformed to his views of how a wife should be.

She always yearned for appreciation and validation from him, which she never received until he lived.

When she was sixty-eight, her husband was diagnosed with cancer. She did everything she could to manage the restaurant and take care of him. That's when she decided to reduce the menu to fewer items to make it manageable.

But two years later, when she was seventy, she decided to close the restaurant after her husband's death. One day, a customer walked in. She shared with him the news of closing the restaurant. After a long silence, the customer responded sadly, 'I'll never be able to eat this ramen again.'

This one sentence made her rethink her move. She decided to continue with the thought that there are people who look forward to eating her ramen.

'I need to cook for myself, anyway. So why not make a little more, for as long as I can, to serve the customers who want to eat my ramen?' she thought. Then, she decided to continue to run the restaurant with just two of her most popular dishes in the menu. She wanted to have a balance, so she reduced the opening days of the restaurant to five days a week. Every time she finds it hard to keep up, she remembers a satisfied look of a customer eating her food, and that motivates her to get back to doing it. She believes if one decides to do something, the body will cooperate—*yaro to omottara yareru.*

The restaurant is just an extension of her house., It has two seats at the bar counter and one communal table with four seats. It has a very homely ambience.

The menu consists of only two items: gyoza and ramen. Masako-san's ramen is renowned for its special broth, made from chicken and pork bones with marrow, ten different vegetables and seafood, simmered together for thirteen hours. She even makes the gyoza skins from scratch!

Running the restaurant single-handedly, Masako-san takes care of everything—from cooking to cleaning and sourcing raw materials. Despite not having much money, she finds happiness in the way she operates the restaurant, with just two items on the menu. Her two sons are neither interested in taking over nor helping her; they want her to quit. But she remains determined to continue.

When asked if she feels sad being alone after her husband's death, she responded that instead of thinking what she couldn't do without him around, she has started to concentrate on what she can. In fact, now that he is no longer around, it has helped her pursue her own interests. She mentioned that her husband never allowed her to dance or wear pretty clothes. So now, at the age of seventy-one, she has decided to pursue dancing lessons.

Not being exposed to social life, taking the first step was hard for in the beginning. On the first day of the lesson, she was very shy and equally embarrassed that she couldn't even perform simple moves. At the end of the lesson, she decided to quit.

However, when she got home, she felt sad and thought if there was any other way to get better, without being embarrassed in front of other people.

That's when she had the epiphany: Every one of them on the dance lesson must have been a beginner once. They must've felt the same embarrassment as her. And if she were good on the very first day of the lesson, there would be nothing to look forward to and make improvements for. Moreover, there won't be any satisfaction of getting better either.

'Everyone is a beginner when they start anything new. With that thought in mind, you can start anything at any time. So, don't get intimidated when you see others doing better than you,' she says.

Now, twice a week, she goes to her dance classes and practices almost every day at home. When asked if she gets tired, she says there are days where she cannot take the next step and has to literally crawl out from her bed. But come next day, she drags herself to the lesson. And when the music starts, she somehow gets the energy and cannot stop dancing then.

Her friends often ask her if she has regrets from the past. Her answer? She doesn't, because she did everything she could at that moment with the resources and opportunities she had. According to her, she gave her best to the marriage, and that's why she's able to do what she now does, without any guilt. Some of her widowed friends have regrets that they could've given more to their marriage, but she has no apprehensions of such kind.

Masako-san enjoys engaging in conversations with the restaurant's customers, considering it an essential part of her life. Both the restaurant and dancing keep her alive and fill her with happiness. Despite the challenges of executing difficult dance moves, when the music starts, she forgets all the pain and immerses herself in the joy of dancing. She believes that she is happiest during those moments.

Masako-san's outlook on life remains positive, and she looks forward to what lies ahead. She continually seeks ways to improve her ramen recipe, learn new dance moves, and is excited about the future.

Prof. Hasegawa's Ikigai Expert Commentary

Masako-san has always loved to devote herself fully to whatever she takes up. She has loved to dance since she was a child but never had the opportunity. Because of the strictness of her spouse, she was not allowed to express herself—even in the restaurant they both ran together. Now, she runs the restaurant that her late spouse cherished, but she has also found something new in the form of dancing to devote herself to and spends her days full of vitality.

The death of her spouse created a trigger for Masako-san to feel that she could now find ways to express herself freely and feel alive overcoming the challenges of learning and mastering ballroom dancing, while feeling fulfilled to continue serving the customers of her husband's restaurant and experimenting with new recipes that expressed her creativity. By serving her long-loved ramen and dumpling recipes, it has given her the fulfilment of serving customers. Expressing herself through ballroom dancing has given her joy and made her feel alive.

Acceptance and Commitment Therapy (ACT) is a mindfulness-based behavioural therapy designed to help individuals accept difficult emotions and thoughts, like those arising from past regrets, and focus on taking meaningful actions aligned with their values.[18]

It emphasizes psychological flexibility—the ability to adapt to situations while staying committed to a purpose-driven life. ACT helps you overcome regrets in a variety of ways:

- Acknowledging and accepting feelings of regret without judgment or resistance.
- Recognizing that regret is a natural response and part of being human.
- Learning to separate yourself from regretful thoughts.
- Staying focused on the present, letting go of unhelpful rumination about past actions.
- Observing regretful thoughts without letting them dominate your emotions.
- Identifying what truly matters to you, which can provide a sense of purpose and direction.
- Taking small, purposeful steps toward goals or values, even while carrying the emotional weight of regret.

By directing all your focus and energy on the present, you can start your journey today and move on from past regrets to start activities that make your today more enjoyable. By understanding that no matter what happened in the past, the present is the most important to make every day worth living, prioritize living in the 'here-and-now' to help you let go of past regrets.

Heartfelt advice for you from Masako-san

Instead of focusing on the things you cannot do (victim-mindset), focus on taking the first step and doing things with whatever is accessible to you right now.

We hope that you enjoyed Masako-san's story, and that it triggered some feelings inside you. Allow us to give you a tiny nudge here and now for your own Ikigai365 journey.

Close your eyes and take a deep breath, reflecting on the following question before writing down the answer:

Is there anything you wanted to do in the past, but were prevented from, or could not do? Why? What stopped you?

_____

_____

_____

If Masako-san can, so can you. Take that first step today!

Sidebar: Life Skills From Ballroom Dancing

Ballroom dancing is a wonderful teacher of important life lessons! It highlights the values of communication, partnership, and adaptability.

Partners coordinate seamlessly through non-verbal cues, strengthening teamwork and respect. Regular practice builds perseverance, patience, and a great work ethic. Confidence and presence soar, boosting self-esteem and social skills.

The artistic aspect promotes creativity and living in the moment. Plus, ballroom dancing instils sportsmanship—celebrating victories graciously and bouncing back from setbacks with resilience. It's not just dancing; it's a joyful journey of learning and growing together!

Key quote

'Never be defined by your past. It was just a lesson, not a life sentence.'

Rewire – Don't Retire

Meet Ishizaki-san, the networker!

Life's secret mantra: *Keizoku wa chikara nari*—persistence always pays off.

We often hear that age is just a state of mind. But Ishizaki-san personifies youthful energy, even at eight-three. His zest for life and the zeal to make every conversation count left us craving for more, after more than an hour over coffee at Tokyo Imperial Hotel on a rain-soaked evening.

Ishizaki-san has been building social networks in Japan for decades, beginning in the late-eighties—well before the advent of the internet and social media. He is a real-life personification of a LinkedIn influencer, with a vast network of connections— the only difference is that he has tilled, tended and nurtured this network like growing his own backyard garden.

'Dedicate your life to creating communities where people come together, enjoy each other's company, and find some way to contribute to society,' he says.

When asked what keeps him occupied these days, now that he has long been retired, he looks a bit puzzled. 'Retired?!' he asks, before passionately diving into sharing his passion project Japan Platform, which he has built into a forum for donors looking to support victims of natural disasters.

What started as an idea nearly fifteen years ago has grown big and impactful. The project is clearly still one of his biggest sources of everyday energy and pride, for he is able to make a difference in people's lives. He waxes eloquent about how he tried to make the Japan Platform as big as the Red Cross donations in terms of a network of corporate and individual donors. He took it upon himself as a challenge to ensure there would be a sustained source of funding each time there was a natural disaster. This was aimed to complement the development assistance and provide immediate relief to those impacted on the ground. He has on his fingertips the specifics of when, how, and the amount they mobilized for Fukushima, Ukraine, Turkey, and the challenges each of them posed.

He is filled with pure gratitude for his nearly fifty-years-long professional career that he looks back upon fondly, as it has helped him build the foundation of a very vast network, serving his past customers, suppliers, and colleagues. He served as the branch manager at Mitsubishi Bank, where he helped a wide variety of locals and businesses, and is quick to acknowledge that 'bowing down my head to say "Thank you" to every one of them was my real investment in building my network.'

During the latter half of his career, he greatly benefited from the wisdom and counsel as Chief of Staff of the fourth generation Mitsubishi group founder. One advice he took to heart and lives by the mantra is to give more, take less.

After tirelessly dedicating his professional life to his employers, including 150 hours overtime in a month, Ishizaki-san decided to 'switch gears' instead of 'retiring' in his late-sixties. He wanted to meet many different people, find new—both challenging and exciting—ways of helping people in his network and spend time learning, immersing in a couple of his passion areas: Japanese *sake* and Japanese art galleries.

His passion for sake took an interesting turn, when the Fukushima earthquake-tsunami dual-disaster of 2011 rendered hundreds of local sake breweries fighting for survival. After volunteering in the ravaged area—his 'networking DNA' led him to start regular monthly get-togethers of fellow volunteers in his locality. These meetings initially began as chit-chats over various types of Japanese sake, but he noticed that the group slowly started expanding—as people brought in more of their own network of friends and colleagues and these evolved into 'monthly sake tasting sessions' which till today run. 'We just finished our 107th session,' he says.

Ishizaki-san observed that when people are enjoying themselves—eating, drinking, and having a good time—they are more willing to give. At the end of every event, whether it's an art gallery or a sake gathering, he places a donation box, and their happiness often leads to genuine generosity.

Over the years, these sake group sessions have become expert tasting (wine sommelier-like) rating sessions for local sake breweries from all over Japan. The knowledge and passion flows, as he narrates the specific top brands and breweries in different prefectures and who moved up or down, compared to last year.

We asked Ishizaki-san to share his secret formula for energy and youthfulness, and how he takes care of his health at this age, while managing the stress of running the platform and keeping in touch with his network.

'Sleep early, sleep enough, sleep at regular times, and wake up early,' he replies. He wakes up at 4 a.m., he tells us. 'Walk around and take the stairs as much as possible,' he adds. He says he walks 15,000 to 20,000 steps daily. He also makes time to take a short afternoon nap—*hirune*—wherever he may be.

He also insists that his love for Japan Platform and networking means it is not a source of stress, as it is helping others and keeping him socially active and connected. But he does share his philosophy of how he does not allow stress to accumulate, which has something to do with his relationship with god. Most of us visit religious places to pray and ask for things, but Ishizaki-san goes to a temple whenever he is stressed, talks to God, and hands over all his troubles to him. This helps him prevent stress from piling up.

His dream is someday to make 'every single gathering of people in Japan', not just a fun event for bonding and networking, but the one that ends with 'giving to charity' to help others.

At eighty-three years of age, the combination of Ishizaki-san's energy, zest, simplicity, and clarity offers a role model to living every day with a sense of feeling alive and making every single conversation 'count' to strengthen relationships and trust. He doesn't believe in the concept of 'retiring' and rather believes that transitioning to a phase of self-care, getting out every day to interact with the outside world, so that there is *karui shigeki*—moderate stimuli—to keep him challenged and to learn by bonding and networking to find ways to lead a more fulfilling life.

Prof. Hasegawa's Ikigai Expert Commentary

When I read Ishizaki-san's story, I was immediately struck how it really doesn't matter whether it's sake, or whether it's art, or whether it's the donor's part of the story—these are all just different ways for him to create a *butai* (stage) for people to come together and becomes an opportunity for networking. His motivation appears to be building a variety of these stages for people to come together and interact over various activities.

While many people struggle to find activities outside of work—especially after retirement—Ishizaki-san has effortlessly devoted himself to vigorous activities and blurring the lines between past relationships made at work and other activities outside work. He has an intense passion for creating immersive experiences and making new discoveries as well as connections born out of the need for 'stimulation' of his curiosity. The act of bringing people together to enjoy each other's company, while contributing to society, gives him tremendous satisfaction and a strong feeling of accomplishment.

The principle of reciprocity is a foundational concept in social psychology, describing the social norm that dictates that people respond to each other's actions with similar actions— whether positive or negative. In networking, the act of giving back is often driven by the desire to reciprocate for past favours or to build goodwill for future collaboration. Creating spaces for interaction allows individuals to practice and reinforce reciprocity, contributing to stronger social ties and collaborative efforts.[19]

By creating opportunities for people to network and give back, you tap into the natural human instinct to reciprocate, fostering a cycle of generosity and mutual support that strengthens communities and networks.

It is important to remember that work is only a means of earning an income, and earning money is not the purpose of life. Rather, the sense of belonging, fulfilment, and accomplishment truly gives value to one's life. Start with things you enjoy (like sake made Ishizaki-san feel alive), take small first steps rightaway to use that as a springboard to interact with other people (like Ishizaki-san found like-minded people who wanted to help sake breweries suffering from the Tohoku earthquake-tsunami.)

Start doing this regularly together to create a group/network that bonds together when they come together to support and benefit others, without worrying about making a big impact and leaving a legacy.

Heartfelt advice for you from Ishizaki-san

Life's biggest treasures are relationships and connections with other people. And all the various roles we play in life are meaningless unless they lead to deep and trusting relationships.

We hope that you enjoyed Ishizaki-san's story, and it triggered some feelings inside you. Allow us to give you a tiny nudge here and now for your own Ikigai365 journey.

You may wish to use the tool 'Letter from Future Self' in myIkigai365 Nourishment Journal.

Close your eyes and take a deep breath, reflecting on the following questions before writing down the answers:

When was the last time you gave something without any expectation of receiving anything in return? When is the next time you will do this again?

_____

_____

_____

Has anyone ever given anything to you without any expectations of getting something in return? How did it make you feel?

_____

_____

_____

If Ishizaki-san can, so can you. Take that first step today!

Sidebar: Four Phases of Retirement

Dr Riley Moynes outlines the four phases of retirement based on his research and personal experience on his TED talk:

Phase I—Vacation mode: This phase is filled with excitement and freedom. Retirees enjoy newfound time for relaxation and activities they couldn't pursue before.

Phase II—Loss and disenchantment: After the honeymoon phase, many retirees feel a loss of purpose. They experience identity shifts and miss the structure, social connection, and purpose that work provided.

Phase III—Trial and error: Retirees begin searching for new ways to fill their time and find meaning. They try different hobbies, volunteer work, or part-time jobs, experimenting with how to stay engaged.

Phase IV—Reinvention and fulfilment: The final phase is where retirees find their stride, often rediscovering purpose in new roles, passions, or community involvement, leading to a rewarding and fulfilling retirement.

Key quote

'My father said there were two kinds of people in the world: givers and takers. The takers may eat better, but the givers sleep better.'

—Marlo Thomas Yo

'Somehow . . . It All Works Out'

Meet Kunimitsu-san and Noriko-san!

Life's secret mantra: *Nantoka narudesho*—somehow it will all work out.

Let me start with a question: Have you ever come across a couple who tease each other in a playful manner, yet still display deep affection?

Upon our initial encounter with Kunimitsu-san, aged eighty-one and Noriko-san, aged seventy-six, we were amazed by their youthful approach. This couple truly embodies the notion that age is merely a number. They both looked well-groomed—wore crisp shirts, neatly pressed trousers, and clean shoes, all while radiating a happiness that made them seem younger than they were. Not a single day seemed to have passed beyond their sixties.

At sixty-eight, when Kunimitsu-san officially entered retirement, this concept seemed foreign to him. The way he transitioned from being employed full-time to retirement is something is worth mentioning. In the final three years leading up to his retirement—at the age of sixty-five—he gradually reduced his workdays, progressing from five days a week to four, then three, two, and eventually just one day. This allowed both him and Noriko-san to gradually adapt to this new way of life.

When we asked him about how his company had responded to his decision, he replied with a smile, stating that they had no other choice but to support his decision; otherwise, he would have resigned anyway. He also emphasized the importance of individuals upskilling themselves to become indispensable within their workplaces.

Kunimitsu-san consistently involves himself in various activities that interest him. He possesses a strong passion for continuous learning, exemplified by his regular engagement in golf, which helps keep his mind sharp. He intentionally plays with different groups each time to expand his social circle and meet newer individuals. He is also a Kendo master, which is one of the reasons behind his fit mind and body.

On the other hand, Noriko-san finds joy in creating beautiful works of art. When asked about her love for art, she modestly retrieves three postcard-size paper sheets from her folder and offers them to us to have a look. To our surprise, the artwork displayed on those pages depicted beautiful Japanese landmarks, such as the Sensoji Temple, Tokyo National Museum, and Tokyo Station.

When asked if she sells her art pieces, she responded that she has no such desire. For her, the process of making art brings happiness to her heart, and she has no intention of parting with her creations. In addition to this interest, she also loves to take care of the flowers in her garden, beaming with joy each time she looks at them.

Kunimitsu-san and Noriko-san truly embody an inspiring couple dynamic. They actively participate in *tabearuki*, a group activity where people explore different places and enjoy meals together. Moreover, Kunimitsu-san possesses a deep fascination with history and mythology, and has currently dedicating himself to researching Momotaro, the Japanese legend.

When asked about it, he started explaining. Often referred to as 'Peach Boy', Momotaro is a beloved Japanese folklore passed down through generations. He was discovered as a baby inside a giant peach by an elderly childless couple in a river, who later raised him as their own son. Momotaro symbolizes bravery, virtue, and the triumph of good over evil. In this traditional tale, he sets out to defeat ogres (demons) causing chaos and is depicted as a courageous character aided by loyal animal companions.

A number of variations for it exist in the story, as it is retold in children's books, movies, and plays to cater to diverse audiences. In one of them, Momotaro is portrayed as a thug and thief, no different from the demons he fought. These demons had stolen treasures from poor townspeople, and he, rather than returning the items, brought them back to his parents. Despite such variations, a Momotaro statue remains a symbol at Okayama station.

Kunimitsu-san has written a research paper on his findings on Momotaro. During their joint pursuit, him and Noriko-san embark on visits to ancient tombs, allowing him to conduct his research while she joyfully accompanies him, taking pleasure in the opportunity to try new cuisines. It wouldn't be incorrect to suggest that Kunimitsu-san's current Ikigai revolves around his Momotaro research. As a result, there appears to be a notable convergence of their respective Ikigai, further strengthening their bond.

Observing their remarkable chemistry, we couldn't help but ask about how they handle differences and conflicts as a couple. As we posed the question, their gazes met, as if engaging in silent conversation, and then Kunimitsu-san shared their approach. He revealed that in such situations, they choose to disengage and redirect their focus, effectively avoiding further arguments.

When asked for advice on marriage, she responds with a smile. Then, she emphasizes on the importance of maintaining individual hobbies—even if they differ for each partner. 'As long as there is a solid foundation, the family will thrive,' she says. She further suggests prioritizing financial stability as a baseline, as it sets the stage for everything else to fall into place.

Naturally, our curiosity leads us to ask how they define stability, and how much is enough for a family. She explains that as long as her basic needs are met, she is willing to forgo her own wants. However, when it comes to their children, she desires to save for their wants as well. Listening to his wife's wise words, Kunimitsu-san adds that respecting each other's interests is crucial for a harmonious relationship. He also emphasizes the importance of avoiding excessive nagging, complaining, or interfering in each other's lives.

Our curiosity deepened as we tried to understand how they had developed such profound insights about family and relationships. She shared that both of them had to travel to several countries, including the US, due to Kunimitsu-san job which had greatly influenced her perspective. The experiences had opened her up, prompting her to let go of trivial matters that can often strain relationships. It won't be wrong to say that the Kaizuka couple are global citizens. Their open-mindedness and eagerness to embrace new influences make them true citizens of the world. They possess a remarkable ability to swiftly learn and adapt, allowing them to navigate various cultures and environments with ease.

What distinguishes this charming couple goes beyond their remarkable approach to handling situations and their mutual support for each other's interests is their deep-rooted belief in the Japanese philosophy of *nantoka narudesho*, which translates to 'somehow it will work out'. This belief serves as a guiding principle for them, instilling a sense of optimism and resilience in the face of challenges.

Kunimitsu-san and Noriko-san's love is a beacon of hope, inspiring us all to treasure the beauty of a love that blossoms with age.

Prof. Hasegawa's Ikigai Expert Commentary

The Kaizuka couple both lived through Japan's period of rapid economic growth in the 1960s, followed by spending several years abroad for work in the 1970s. Even after nearly five decades, they now speak of those times as if the memories are still fresh, recognizing and reminiscing how those experiences continue to shape who they are today.

Kunimitsu-san and Noriko-san's life together almost echoes the spirit of Ueki Hitoshi's song, 'Damatte Ore Ni Tuite Koi' (Don't Speak, Follow Me). However, this also shows no matter how painful the past might be, it also eventually passes and the pain fades away.

Kunimitsu-san began his journey with kendo during his elementary school years, and it didn't take long for him to become deeply passionate about it. But now, many decades later, his interests have shifted. He continues to enjoy learning new things, with his current passions focused on golf and the traditional Japanese folktale of Momotaro. Noriko-san, too, likes to fill her days drawing beautiful landscapes, caring for her plants, and exploring curiously the world around her. Occasionally, they play a round of golf together as a couple. As they have always valued each other's hobbies, they find ways to spend time together while still embracing their own personal interests. And by immersing themselves in these, they feel a sense of comfort, enjoyment, and fulfilment.

According to the Cognitive Adaptation Theory, over time, people adapt to adversity by finding meaning, regaining control, and fostering self-esteem.[20] Time enables reframing of past negative events, making them less painful and more comprehensible.

We can observe both of them striving to find positive meaning even in the negativity from the past. Even if the bygones remind them of unpleasant events like the fights they had, their move abroad to New York, where it was tough to be a foreigner, they choose to look past these and prefer making their present pleasant by broadening their current realities and shrinking the past.

This letting-go of the past and prioritizing feeling-good present requires making the here-and-now our most important focus in life. The more we do this, the more things start resolving themselves and changing for the better with time. Believing in the healing power of time is the foundation of their *nantoka naru deshou* philosophy—that somehow, it all works out.

Heartfelt advice for your from Kaizuka couple

'Differences and conflicts are bound to happen in every marriage. In such events, one should choose to disengage and redirect their focus, effectively avoiding further arguments.'

– Kunimitsu-san

'It is very important to maintain your individual hobbies, even if they differ from your partner's. As long as there is a solid foundation, the family will thrive.'

—Noriko-san

We hope that you enjoyed the Kaizuka couple's story, and it triggered some feelings inside you. Allow us to give you a tiny nudge here and now for your own Ikigai365 journey.

Close your eyes and take a deep breath, reflecting on the following question before writing down the answer:

What do you do every day for the people who matter the most in your life, to make them feel needed, cared for, and accepted as they are?

_____

_____

_____

If the Kaizuka couple can, so can you. Take that first step today!

Sidebar: Dynamics of Japanese couples

Have you ever wondered how Japanese couples typically manage their relationships?

Traditionally, in a Japanese household, the man is usually the main earner, and the woman takes care of the home and manages the family's finances.

The husband often works long hours in demanding jobs, focusing on earning money for the family. Because of his job, he might not spend much time at home.

On the other hand, the wife handles household chores like cooking, cleaning, and taking care of the children. She also manages the family's budget, including paying bills and saving money. Even if she has a job, she is still expected to manage the household finances. There is an interesting term, *okozukai*, which translates to 'pocket money' or 'allowance' that a Japanese wife gives to her husband.

The concept is quite practical and specific. It is the husband's personal spending money, separate from the household budget. He uses this money for his daily expenses, such as commuting, buying lunch, getting haircuts, and occasionally enjoying a drink. This system ensures that the family's main income is managed efficiently, while still providing the husband with some financial autonomy for his personal needs.

When married men in Japan socialize with other married men, they often discuss how much okozukai they receive. Isn't this interesting?

There is a Japanese phrase, '*Te no hira de korogasu*' (手のひらで転がす) that translates to 'rolling something in the palm of one's hand'.

In the context of relationships, particularly with couples in Japan, this phrase is often used figuratively to describe someone who can manipulate or control their partner with ease. It has a subtle, playful, or sometimes negative connotation, depending on how it's used.

Key quote

'A great marriage is not when the perfect couple comes together, it's when an imperfect couple learns to enjoy their differences.'

My Life. My Pace. My Stage. My Sanctuary

Meet Teraguchi-san!

Life's secret mantra: 'You are special in your own way. Be yourself, and don't get too caught up in opinions of other people or societal expectations.'

Unlike the regular ones, the entrance of Danke Cafe is rather simple: a black signboard and tinted glass. Upon opening the door and stepping inside, instead of the typical atmosphere of a cafe commonly seen in Japan, the shelves are adorned with beautifully crafted coffee cups from the famous Okura Ceramic Studio. Despite the dim lighting, there's a subtly bright atmosphere, and when you take a seat at the bar, Teraguchi-san warmly greets us with a cheerful expression. Soon, with the rich aroma of coffee, heartfelt conversations unfold.

Danke was founded by Teraguchi-san in 1977. This is a specialty coffee shop specializes in hand-drip coffee using Melitta drippers, continuing to utilize the filter drip technology and culture developed by the Germans who invented the first ever coffee filter. In gratitude and respect for Melitta Bentz, who played a significant role in this development, and overall popularization of the coffee culture, the cafe was named Danke—German for 'thanks'.

When Teraguchi-san decided to open his own cafe, he was determined to create a truly unique and special experience for his customers. He handpicked every aspect of his shop—right from the expensive Okura pottery coffee cups and the glassware to the cutlery and coffee grinders. Most of the Okura cups are limited editions, costing some hundred thousand yen each. Each cup of coffee is customized—Teraguchi-san even chooses which cup to serve each customer's coffee in! He values years of experience, sensory insight, and intuitive judgment to decide.

Imagine our delight when we found ourselves sipping from a stunning sakura-patterned cup, and our visit to the cafe was right after a stroll through the blossoms in the nearby park. Curiosity piqued, we did a quick online search, only to discover that one of the cups in our hands was priced at 556,000 yen. Taken aback by its value, we couldn't help but voice our concern about the risk of breakage. But with a reassuring smile, he says, 'The value lies not in the cup, but in the shared experience of the person enjoying the coffee. The customer drinking the coffee is far more valuable than any material object. If it were to break, it would have fulfilled its purpose.' And true to his word, not a single cup has ever been broken by the hands of a customer. Any breakage, he admits, has always been his own doing.

He takes great care to roast and grind the beans right before brewing. His way of brewing coffee, wrapping each cup in both hands, and making it with closed eyes like a prayer, is both impressive and mystical, resembling a sacred ceremony—anyone who witnesses it can't look away. Through the lengthy brewing process, he seeks to convey gratitude, love, and wishes happiness and blessings to the customer before serving it.

It is clear that he takes great pride in every cup he serves. He serves not only delicious coffee, but also a sense of warmth and connection that is truly unique. His passion for coffee runs deep, so much so that he wishes to pass away while pouring a cup.

The highlight of Danke is its butter-blended coffee. It has a reputation for its unique secret method, where butter permeates the hot coffee beans immediately after roasting, bringing out rich flavours and aromas. Talking about this special blend, he gave us a butter-blended coffee bean to chew. The bean exuded the aroma of dark chocolate mixed with the natural scent of butter. Upon biting into the bean, the slight saltiness of the butter enhanced the coffee's original flavour like a seasoning, making it even richer.

Teraguchi-san's passion for coffee began since his student days. Eventually, he worked for a major coffee company but ventured into the cafe business in Kobe while still being employed. Initially, butter blended coffee wasn't offered at his cafe.

The early days of Danke saw typical roasting of about seven types of single-origin and blended beans, each roasted to accentuate its unique characteristics. Back then, as black coffee drinkers were few, the common practice was to use coffee creamer and sugar. However, an issue arose when its use would cloud the coffee's colour and taste. Searching for a solution, he discovered—through literature, of all things—that in England, milk is added to coffee to soften its taste, and that people enjoyed sugar coffee during the American Westward Expansion. The Boston Tea Party incident of 1773 had led to a shift in American drinking culture from tea to coffee. During their travels, settlers carried coffee beans and roasted them frequently. However, this would easily lead to oxidation, spoiling the taste. To prevent this, roasted beans were coated with sugar immediately after to preserve the flavour. Thus came the name 'sugar coffee'.

Taking cues from what he read, Teraguchi-san sought a way to express the flavour of coffee, but without using milk or cream, all while maintaining its depth and smoothness. After four years of trial and error, he noticed that butter, with its low moisture content, resembled the texture of coffee oils, and that using it resulted in a richer taste.

The experiment was a resounding success: The coffee he created had a milky smoothness similar to cream, but without the oiliness of butter floating on top.

Danke's butter-blended coffee, which debuted when Teraguchi-san was twenty-eight years old, was born out of this process. He promptly removed all existing coffee offerings, staking the cafe's fortunes solely on butter-blended coffee. The result was a great success. Rumours of 'delicious coffee' and 'unique coffee' spread, leading people to flock to the café. Soon, rivals began to emulate his butter-blended coffee. However, Teraguchi-san didn't get bothered by such imitations; instead, he saw them as validation. As a result, his fan base only grew thicker, and for the past forty-three years, his cafe has served only this special blend.

The process of making butter-blended coffee is labour-intensive. Immediately after roasting, the coffee beans are coated with butter. If not done promptly, the coffee's get covered with an oily layer. The success of this step determines the outcome. Therefore, the choice of coffee beans for blending, and the timing and amount of butter used, remain Teraguchi-san's trade secret.

Operating a coffee shop with just one type of coffee is a risky move—both today and in the past. It takes confidence and patience, but most importantly, a real love for coffee, as he believes passion is what keeps a business going. While financial stability is crucial for livelihood, he emphasizes the significance of this intrinsic motivation.

'When you really love something, even if it's hard, it doesn't feel like work. I enjoy what I do because I love it,' he says.

When asked what one should do if they're not passionate about anything, he compares it to an arranged marriage. 'Even if you're not immediately in love, you should try to make an effort to like it, just like you would try to impress someone you want to fall in love with you,' he says. 'Even if you don't start out loving it, with effort, you might end up liking it, just like falling in love.'

Teraguchi-san's passions extend far beyond making exceptional coffee. His favourite pastime involves frequenting bookstores to checkout new arrivals, while also reading an impressive five to seven books each week.

But that's not it—he isn't satisfied by merely absorbing their content. He also proudly showcases his latest collections at the café, with a weekly refresh to the display. What truly sets him apart, however, is his generosity. During conversations with his customers, if he thinks a particular book from his extensive collection can benefit them, he graciously donates it. Encouraging a cycle of knowledge sharing, he then suggests they pass it on to someone else in need.

Teraguchi-san's love for words led him to meticulously compile his favourite quotes, ideas, and insights gained from both books and customer interactions. He freely distributes self-published compilations of these treasures to those who may need inspiration.

His ultimate goal? To create a positive and uplifting atmosphere for his customers. Often, he takes time to talk to his customers and offer life advice over a cup of coffee. Known for his kindness and wisdom, many regular customers visit his cafe specifically to seek his advice.

However, no matter how famous the customer is, Teraguchi-san refrains from initiating conversations until they engage first. He believes that this silence is a sign of respect and empathy for the customer's comfort, and thus maintaining a respectful distance acknowledges and respects their perspective. However, once a customer poses a question, he responds earnestly. Understanding the constraints of time and conversation, he makes an attempt to address even the smallest inquiries with genuine sincerity.

Teraguchi-san's coffee shop is more than just a place to grab a cup of coffee. It's a sanctuary where customers can forget their worries and concerns and find a moment of peace and quiet. From the soothing ambiance to the personal touch he brings to every cup of coffee he serves, his goal is to create a special place where customers can truly unwind and take a break from the stress of daily life. He wants his customers to leave his cafe feeling better than how they did when they walked in, and to have a memorable experience they will want to come back to.

Prof. Hasegawa's Ikigai Expert Commentary

Teraguchi-san has lived his whole life with an extraordinary commitment to bringing out the best coffee flavour and taste. He feels a sense of satisfaction and fulfilment when he sees a smile on the faces of his customers. He especially enjoys creating subtle interactions between various elements of his coffee shop.

Through his coffee shop, Teraguchi-san has created a one-of-a-kind existence for himself. The café is a like a place where one can listen to the 'sound of silence'. The interaction between the coffee and Teraguchi-san, between him and his customers, and the one between the furnishings in the space and him, as well as the objects in the store, the people there, and the interaction of each element—from the past, to the present, and the future—are all enclosed within this one space.

All of it makes this feel like sanctuary to his regular customers.

The Japanese saying '*Iwanu ga hana*' (What is left unsaid is the flower) refers to not telling the whole story intentionally, because by doing so, it would make the charm stand out, thus make the storytelling seem quainter. Just as a flower is appreciated for its beauty without an explanation, certain emotions or sentiments are also more powerful when left unsaid, trusting the other person to 'see the flower' on their own and feel the 'symbolism of the unspoken'.

The power of implied meaning can be observed in the field of Gestalt psychology. The word 'gestalt' is German for 'structure' or 'form' and refers to a unified structure with a sense of wholeness. Gestalt is a school of psychology that attempts to understand the human psyche not as a collection of parts and elements, but with an emphasis on the wholeness and structure. According to the Gestalt psychology, especially Max Wertheimer's Law of Organization, the human mind seeks to fill in information gaps. When something is left unsaid, it invites interpretation, engaging the imagination and emotions of the listener. This aligns with iwanu ga hana by suggesting that leaving things unspoken can deepen connections by allowing others to interpret the underlying intent in their own way.

This power of *chinmoku* (沈黙) creates an environment for silent observation. This idea emphasizes that answers lie in the invisible, and hence pausing in the present creates space for emotions to surface, making conversations become something where more is felt than said. It is interestingly similar to appreciating coffee based on how you feel, instead of trying to describe it in words.

I associate this with how Teraguchi-san experiences his life at the coffee shop. His café is a space where he creates an environment that is conducive to activating the agency of his customers. The space is not only a physical sanctuary, but also an emotional one, which facilitates a brief pause for his customers to feel refreshed and recharged.

Personally, we feel like visiting and listening to the silence in such a space. Do you?

Heartfelt advice for you from Teraguchi-san

Always do the right thing. Your heart will never lie to you about taking the right path or decision, even in difficult stations. It is very easy to stray from this and justify it by hiding behind others' opinions. But all you are doing is escaping reality, and something you will likely regret later.

We hope you found inspiration in Teraguchi-san's story. Here's a small invitation to start exploring your own Ikigai365 path.

Close your eyes and take a deep breath, reflecting on the following question before writing down the answer:

Reflect on a decision you recently made which continues to bother you. Was it because you didn't follow your heart? Did you get carried away by others' justification?

_____

_____

_____

If Teraguchi-san can, so can you. Take that first step today!

Sidebar: Coffee Culture in Japan

Coffee culture in Japan is rich and multifaceted, blending traditional local elements with global trends.

Coffee was first introduced to Japan by Dutch traders in the seventeenth century, but it didn't get popular until the late nineteenth and early-twentieth centuries. The original Japanese coffee shop came to be called a *kissaten*, usually described as a no-rush place to grab a bite and something to drink. The word is loosely translated as a tea-room but which also serves coffee. The first official kissaten, Kahi Chakan, was established in 1888 in Ueno. Nowadays, coffee shops are commonly referred to as cafes, and using the term kissaten suggests a more vintage-styled coffee establishment.

Many kissaten are known for their meticulous hand-drip coffee, prepared with great care and attention to detail. There are certain blends of coffee that are very popular in Japan, like the Blue Mountain coffee of Jamaica, whose 65–80 per cent of global production is exported to the Asian country.

Coffee culture in Japan is a fascinating blend of traditional and modern elements, with a deep appreciation for quality, craftsmanship, and innovation.

Key quote

Ishindenshin (以心伝心) implies 'heart to heart'. It means sharing your heart's true emotions to connect with someone else.

Short Story

Fragility of Life Fuels
Spirit of Innovation

Meet Yano-san!

Hideo Yano is a remarkable individual who has faced numerous challenges throughout his life, but has always maintained an unwavering spirit of perseverance and resilience. After graduating as a management student, he joined a shipping company at the age of twenty-two, gradually working his way up in the marketing department.

However, Hideo-san's curiosity led him to explore other departments. Eventually, he learned design, despite lacking an engineering background.

After a few years, Hideo-san realized that his innovative ideas were not fully appreciated, and that there was limited room for his creativity within the organization. Determined to explore new avenues and broaden his horizons, he made the decision to quit his job and at the age of thirty-five. This was when Hideo-san embarked on his entrepreneurial journey by starting his own company.

However, his initial ventures were met with failure. This led him to question his abilities. But rather than giving up, Hideo-san decided to change his mindset. He recognized the value of failure as a learning experience and realized that it was an essential part of personal growth. By viewing failure as an opportunity for improvement, he was able to find the motivation to continue pursuing his dreams.

To keep himself motivated and overcome challenges, Hideo-san developed a unique metaphorical system: He imagined a huge closet with different drawers, each representing his past experiences, failures, and knowledge he has gained and stored in them. Whenever he encounters a problem, he mentally accesses these drawers to search for solutions. Additionally, he finds his inspiration in nature, often taking walks in the mountains or by the sea. Hideo-san believes that being immersed in the beauty of nature has helped forget his worries and provided him with a fresh perspective.

Despite the obstacles he faced, Hideo-san's determination and innovative spirit led him to obtain six patents in his name, and now, he runs a successful business.

But around five years ago, his journey took an unexpected turn, when he was diagnosed with cancer. This setback did not discourage him, but instead, he used it as a wake-up call. Recognizing the fragility of life, he became even more determined to make the most of every moment and work harder to achieve his goals.

Currently in remission, Hideo-san started another company last year and continues to explore new business opportunities. His experiences with cancer have reinforced his belief that one must never give up. He sees his battle with cancer as a reminder of the urgency to accomplish more and leave a lasting impact on the world. Hideo-san remains hopeful, thankful for the lessons he has learned, and eager to continue trying out new things. He remains open to exploring new opportunities and businesses, firmly believing that if he doesn't give up, his body will respond and support him in achieving his goals.

His determination, the attitude towards embracing failure, and the enduring spirit of an entrepreneur are simply amazing.

Short Story

Kimono-Inspired Vitality

Meet Megumi-san!

Megumi-san's life took an unexpected turn when, at the age of forty-four, she lost her husband. Suddenly finding herself as a widow, with two school-going children, she faced not only the emotional burden of grief but also the daunting challenge of providing for her family.

Being a homemaker until that point, Megumi-san found herself in the difficult position of having to earn a living. Then, she turned to her lifelong interest in sewing, deciding to pursue it further.

Megumi-san inherited solid skills from her mother. At a time when the Japanese still wore kimonos in their daily lives, her mother had learned authentic French fashion and dressmaking techniques from her aunt, the wife of the French Consul General, and tailored haute couture. Megumi-san's clothes were all handmade by her mother from an early age, and her shoes were made to order. She still remembers the memory of being taken by her mother to the French Consul General's house.

Eventually, her mother opened a dressmaking school, and then went on to study Ito-style dressmaking in earnest at a junior college. It was also around this time that she learned the craft of tea ceremony, flower arrangement, and Japanese as well as French cooking.

After marriage, as Megumi-san's skills improved, she began stitching clothes for her neighbours, drawing upon her creativity and passion for the craft. What truly set her apart was her ability to transform traditional Kimonos into stylish, western clothing. Her unique talent caught the attention of those around her, and the word about her exceptional work spread quickly.

With her reputation growing, Megumi-san started receiving orders from those who wanted her to recreate their old Kimonos with fond memories into fashionable pieces. Her business thrived as more people sought out. Soon, she also started creating unique dresses, suits, table runners, bags, etc. using kimono fabrics.

Despite her success, Megumi-san never stopped learning and exploring new things. She recognized the importance of education and wanted to provide her children with the best opportunities. Motivated by this, she embarked on her own journey of learning English and encouraged her children to follow suit. She worked hard as an international volunteer for thirty years, sharing elements of Japanese culture, such as cooking and kimonos. She says that having fun with foreigners helped her to forget the sadness and loneliness of losing her husband.

Now, Megumi-san, at the age of seventy-seven, continues to embody vitality and positivity. Each day, she practices yoga and meditation along with thirty minutes of learning English—a practice she has maintained for the past four decades. Megumi-san is deeply engaged with her community; she has a flourishing garden that provides her with fresh vegetables which she shares with her neighbours and friends.

Driven by her own experiences as a single mother, Megumi-san extends her empathy to other women facing similar challenges. She selflessly offers free sewing lessons to single mothers, and sometimes entertains them with tea ceremonies, empowering them with both skills and support. Amid the Covid-19 pandemic, Megumi-san once again showcased her caring spirit. Recognizing the scarcity of masks, she utilized her sewing expertise to craft cloth masks and distributed them for free to anyone she encountered.

Megumi-san firmly believes in the importance of gratitude, caring for one another, and that a simple act of kindness can have a profound impact on others. Her unwavering commitment to personal growth, dedication to her family's well-being, resilience, and genuine concern for others make her an inspiring human being, full of kindness.

Short Story

Learning ∞ Sharing Cycle
Drives Youthfulness

Meet Yasuo-san!

His scepticism about the traditional education system led him to pursue a different path after graduating from school. Instead of focusing on academics, he chose blue-collar jobs that allowed him to gain practical skills and support his family. Working diligently, he raised his two children and ensured their successful transition into their own careers.

Yasuo-san's decision to learn English was driven by his fascination with history, particularly the events surrounding World War II. Until then, his access to information was limited to the Japanese perspective, due to his inability to read other scripts. However, he believed that by learning English, he could delve deeper into the history of the war through English books and gain a broader understanding of the global perspective.

Yasuo-san was always intrigued by English-speaking YouTubers, and felt that learning the language would enable him to connect with people from around the world. He saw YouTube as a platform where he could share his opinions, experiences, and knowledge, while reaching a wide audience without the need for fame or financial investment.

With the goal of deepening his historical knowledge and becoming a YouTuber, Yasuo-san took the bold step of enrolling in a university to study English as a major at the age of sixty-six. Even though he was surrounded by much younger classmates, most of whom were under the age of twenty, he did not feel intimidated by being an older student who was almost thrice their age.

Yasuo-san's daily routine consisted of attending two classes in the morning, followed by long hours spent in the library. He immersed himself in reading various publications like *The New York Times* as well as encyclopedia, eager to broaden his understanding of the world and improve his language skills.

Despite facing numerous difficulties, he persisted in his efforts. Even with his best efforts, he failed his exams four times. But rather than giving up, he pushed himself to work even harder. His determination paid off, when he finally passed the exams on his fifth attempt.

Filled with a sense of accomplishment and a desire to share his experiences, he decided to start his own YouTube channel, where he shares stories of his perseverance, offers inspiration to both young and old English learners, and provides valuable tips on how to excel in exams. He wanted to provide a platform where individuals could find encouragement, guidance, and a sense of community.

Additionally, he organizes regular reading sessions and discussion groups, fostering an environment where learners could come together, learn from one another, and support each other's language development—and all it for free.

Yasuo-san's generosity extends beyond his online activities. He goes out of his way to help foreigners he encounters in his town, assisting them in navigating conversations and creating a friendly atmosphere.

Through YouTube, he has connected with many people across Japan. Now, he travels to meet them face-to-face, eagerly looking forward to turning online connections into offline ones. Every day, he sends newsletters about current events, his thoughts, and source links to share his perspective. When they meet, these topics spark engaging discussions. The people he meets often support one another in various ways. The common link among them is English, bringing together individuals of all ages—from teenagers to much older adults. Some are learning English for travel, others to study abroad, and some are inspired by their grandchildren's learning journey.

Reflecting on his experiences, Yasuo-san realized that many of his male classmates had passed away, while the women from his class were still alive. Further investigation revealed that the men who lacked social interactions and hobbies had a higher mortality rate. This discovery reinforced his belief in the importance of cultivating relationships and embracing a fulfilling life.

Currently, Yasuo-san cherishes the joy he finds in learning, connecting with others, and sharing his knowledge through his YouTube channel.

Now that you've read all the stories in the 'Autumn' chapter, we invite you to take a moment to explore the IKIGAI365 Reflection > Action Tool below.

It's a gentle way to keep reconnecting with the small sources and feelings of Ikigai in your own life.

Ikigai365 Reflections > Action Tool

(This exercise takes approximately 60 minutes or longer to complete)
(Recommended frequency: Anytime you feel the need to step back/reflect/get a boost)

Here and Now
Present feelings or emotions
you are experiencing

Past memories
or experiences
triggered

Future
hopes or dreams
rekindled

What change
do you
choose to make

Now, what is the one action you will take today or start tomorrow ?

I will _____

_____

_____

_____

Chapter 4 – Winter

In Japan, winter is peaceful and quiet, with snow-covered landscapes shining in simplicity and purity, yet the Red Torii stands strong and resilient, full of life amid the cold, representing both elimination and cleaning-up as the season brings a sense of renewal.

The stories in this chapter, covering people in their nineties, unfold quietly. Each person featured lives at their own pace, making everyday moments count, and simplifying life in their own way.

Curiosity is Ageless

Step into the world of Ogawa-san!

Life's secret mantra: 'Learn to play every day, and play rooted in curiosity, because curiosity never dies.'

Now, try to guess Ogawa-san's age based on the above mantra and three hints below:

Hint #1: Immunity has been her interest since the 1970s, but it was only recently that she took renewed interest in the topic, teaching herself all about it. This led her to finally publish her first book, *What is Immunity*, in 2021.

Hint #2: As we walk into her small but cozy apartment in the suburbs of Tokyo, it feels like stepping into a world of quiet comfort. Though she lives alone, the space doesn't feel empty: it is warm and thoughtfully arranged. Everything has its place, but not strictly—rather, in a way, it reflects her personality. The place feels like an alpine wooden cottage, and the smell of freshly baked bread drifting in from the kitchen awakens our senses.

Hint #3: As she welcomes us in her house, she looks effortlessly elegant in a black floral satin dress, her short hair neatly combed. It's clear she takes time to care for herself. She sits around her study table as she hands out her name-cards and crisp new printed versions of her book. It's a small, but meaningful moment, showing the quiet pride she takes in her work.

Based on the above hints, how old does Ogawa-san feel to you?

Sixty? Seventy? Eighty? Ninety?

Hundred!

She is the first centenarian in this collection of Ikigai365 stories. And wow! Isn't she a role-model in ageing gracefully, being ever curious, and living independently? Ogawa-san is an inspiration for people to remain independent and accountable for their own lives—be it physically, mentally, emotionally, or economically.

Her fuel? Curiosity.

As humans, we often make quick assumptions about how people in their seventies, eighties, or nineties live. So, we were pleasantly surprised to see that even at this age, Ogawa-san stays active and engaged in her daily activities. She continues to cook for herself, does her own laundry and dishes, and keeps up with household tasks.

Though she has a helper who comes in the morning, Ogawa-san still cleans the house all by herself before the said person arrives. She just likes things to be neat when someone comes over!

When we watch her walk, her posture is straight, and she moves with ease. We ask her secret to staying physically active. She simply smiles and tells us that she never skips her daily stretches.

And guess what? She is already on to her new project, which tackles the trends in the pharma industry, analysing what has changed for the better or worse.

At the age of eighty-five, curiosity triggered Ogawa-san's interest in immunity, and at ninety, she decided to write a book— of which, she graciously gives us all personally autographed copies. She refers to the process of writing the book as *benkyou*— Japanese for 'study done for one's own learning'—rather than *kenkyu*, which refers to formal academic research. In saying this, she highlights that her work was more about personal growth and reflection than producing scholarly findings.

On the other side of the coin is a quiet selflessness. As her god-daughter Kamo-san points out, she wrote this book to support her former students—who're now in their sixties—so they could strengthen their immunity and live well into their hundreds.

Her book was originally set to launch in 2020, but then Covid hit. Instead of letting that stop her, she went back to work, updating her research to include ways to support immunity during the pandemic. With this new insight, she eventually published her book, making it even more relevant and valuable.

What's more? She typed up the entire manuscript of the book on her desktop and ordered all reference material as needed online. Hats off to a digitally savvy nonagenarian!

Curiosity also led Ogawa-san to learn oil painting in her early-eighties—three gorgeous paintings that adorn her living room wall are all fruits of her labour. The backstory here is that she was once babysitting the grandkids of her friends', who had gone to art class. Upon being insisted on trying her hand, she, well . . . refused to take no for an answer!

At seventy-one, curiosity even inspired Ogawa-san to learn about Japanese history as a fun way to find topics while spending time chatting with her friends as she entered retirement.

Another few decades ago, in 1968, curiosity helped Ogawa-san make a selfless mid-career switch in her mid-forties. She decided to teach at a woman-only university, and support those who wanted to build their own careers. This was around the time Japan's post-war rebuilding was complete, and the Tokyo Olympics had put a fresh and rising Japan on the global stage. She believed that her country would only progress in the long run if women also became independent and joined the workforce.

Hence, dedicating the next twenty-five years of her life was her way of selflessly working towards this cause. Her motivation to selflessly champion equality of women's rights came from having suffered unfairness during her college days, back when girls were made to study a year longer and write more exams.

In fact, her curiosity about the world emerged around the 1930s, which was also the time when Japan was rapidly evolving through an interplay of 'war + education + democracy'. This had given Ogawa-san the impetus to study Pharmacy in the following decade and make a condition to her would-be-husband that he permit her to work and build a long successful career at the National Institute of Health.

In 1948, at twenty-four, Ogawa-san had an arranged marriage. But her husband, unfortunately, passed away when she was only forty-nine. Hence, she has spent the last fifty years 'technically alone as a widow, but practically surrounded by lots and lots of stimuli from people whose friendship is deeper than blood relations,' along with various challenges that her curiosity has fuelled.

Ogawa-san is filled with gratitude for being lucky to have benefited from unflinching backing of her progressive father and supportive husband—both of whom were pillars of her strength and instrumental in giving her the moral support needed to navigate the various stages of her journey. She never had any kids of her own, but that has never left her without love and support. She tells us that if she ever needs anything, all she has to do is call, and as many as thirty of her former students would show up for her. Even now, one or two visit regularly, bringing her bento meals and spending time with her. When she was in the hospital, they took turns caring for her, making sure she was never alone.

When asked why they remain so devoted, she simply says it's because she always treated them as individuals—encouraging their interests, supporting them in ways she never experienced growing up. She has always given selflessly, and now, as she put it, life is returning that kindness many times over. Even when she was working on her book, a few of her former students stepped in to help with corrections.

By now, you've probably felt the deep and beautiful bond between Ogawa-san and Kamo-san, her god-daughter. The love they share is truly selfless, built on years of care, trust, and unwavering support. Kamo-san visits her often, making sure she's never alone, and always stays connected—no matter how busy life gets.

It is worth mentioning that during our conversation with Ogawa-san, it was Kamo-san who helped bridge the gaps, patiently interpreting and making sure we fully understood what Ogawa-san wanted to share. One could make out that their relation is purely based on genuine affection and a lifelong connection that only grows stronger with time.

We asked Ogawa-san the secret to her good health and longevity. With a humble and sweet smile, she responded, 'I don't really have strong likes or dislikes when it comes to food. I eat anything and everything, but in controlled portions.'

Prof. Hasegawa's Ikigai365 Expert Commentary

Reading Ogawa-san's story, it occurred to me that while the body keeps ageing, the mind, in tandem, does not need to. It made me wonder if the secret to staying healthy, both mentally and physically, as one grows older, is to age with a sense of curiosity like her. In addition to the atmosphere and flavour created by aging, the experiences accumulated by a person's unique experiences throughout their life serves as their most precious treasure.

All of Ogawa-san's life experiences seem to have triggered her curiosity and fuelled her ingenuity. It also helped her overcome the various bitter experiences, especially those that women commonly faced during her youth and working years, leaving her with a strong sense of accomplishment.

It must also be noted that experiencing the sense of accomplishment of overcoming challenges and obstacles is always much stronger, when the motivation comes from within you while contributing to your sense of feeling alive. When she did this to help others—for instance, while writing a book for her students—it also led to her sense of fulfilment.

A study in 2007 focused on the link between curiosity and life satisfaction.[21]

It describes curiosity as a positive psychological trait that drives individuals to seek new experiences and engage with the world. Their key finding was that curiosity not only enhances positive affect and reduces boredom, but correlates with self-actualization, thereby helping individuals feel a deeper sense of purpose. Further, they found that curious people are more likely to experience flow states, moments of complete immersion and joy in an activity.

Curiosity is a great fuel for Ikigai365 journeys. With boundless curiosity, it becomes possible to discover its near-infinite seeds that are created and accumulated throughout our life—from past experiences, present stimuli, and future hopes and dreams—generating the energy to feel alive and fulfilled not only every day, but through the various seasons of life.

Heartfelt advice for you from Ogawa-san

If you pour your heart and soul into learning something new, enjoyment and fulfilment follows naturally. So, what are you curious about learning next?

We hope Ogawa-san's story stirred something powerful inside you! Let's turn that feeling into action—your Ikigai365 journey is ready to begin.

Close your eyes and take a deep breath, reflecting on the following question before writing down the answer:

Is there anything that you are so curious about that you keep learning about it in different ways, never stopping?

_____

_____

_____

You may wish to use the tool 'Design Your Beautiful Day' in myIkigai365 nourishment journal.

If Ogawa-san can, so can you. Take that first step today!

Sidebar: Fuelling your Curiosity

The Five-Dimensional Curiosity Scale (5DCS)[22] is a psychological tool designed to measure the multifaceted nature of curiosity in individuals.

Developed to capture the complexity of this trait, the 5DCS breaks down curiosity into five distinct dimensions:

1. Joyous exploration
2. Deprivation sensitivity
3. Stress tolerance
4. Social curiosity
5. Thrill seeking

Joyous exploration refers to the pleasure derived from learning new things, while deprivation sensitivity pertains to the discomfort of not knowing and the drive to resolve gaps in knowledge. Stress tolerance measures an individual's ability to handle the uncertainty and potential stress that comes with exploring the unknown. The interest in learning about other people and their thoughts and behaviours constitutes social curiosity. Lastly, thrill seeking reflects a penchant for adventurous and risky experiences.

Together, these dimensions provide a comprehensive understanding of curiosity, highlighting how it motivates individuals to seek out new information and experiences in various ways.

Key quote

'Curiosity will conquer fear, even more than bravery will.'

—James Stephens

Giving Feels Like Receiving

Introducing Okamoto-san!

Life's secret mantra: Happiness is not something that happens to you, but it is something that you find on any normal day—everyday!

Have you ever wondered what happens when the life you've always known suddenly feels empty? That's exactly what happened to our centenarian, Okamoto-san.

For most of her life, she was a devoted housewife in a small village, pouring her heart into caring for her husband, children, and grandchildren. Her days were filled with cooking, cleaning, gardening, and making sure her family was always taken care of.

But as her grandchildren grew older and became more independent, she found herself wondering, 'What now?'

What could she do to bring new energy and purpose into her days?

Then one day, she heard about an opportunity to translate Japanese books into braille, a special reading system for blind and visually impaired people. At the age of sixty, she decided to take on a new challenge and stepped into the world of braille translation—an adventure she never expected but soon grew to love. And now, she's been at it for the past forty years.

At the start, she faced challenges, as she had no prior experience in translation. However, when she was seventy-six, she learned to use the computer, which significantly eased the process for her. So far, she has translated around 290 books, covering a wide range of subjects. While she doesn't have a control over the selection of books, she appreciates the diversity it brings to her reading experience and the opportunity to learn new things. Through her translations, she feels a sense of purpose and usefulness, knowing that her work is helping visually impaired individuals access literature. The voluntary work has since become her source of happiness and a means to remain active.

Okamoto-san believes that one doesn't need any special skills or interests to live a fulfilling life. What truly matters is having the mindset to keep searching for things that brighten your day.

Now, you must be wondering: Was she always like this? Did she always wake up looking forward to the day, finding reasons to feel alive in her everyday routine? And more importantly, how can you and I cultivate this attitude in our own lives?

In Japanese, there's a term called *mikka bouzu*, which literally means 'a monk for three days'. It is used to describe a person who can't stick to anything for a long time, or people who get tired of things quickly, or often, quit soon after starting something. The image is of someone who tried to become a monk but quit after three days, because he couldn't handle the training.

Though mikka bouzu has a negative connotation, it can be used in a positive way. Like Okamoto-san believes it's better to be a mikka bouzu, than to not try at all. This way, she thinks, one can try many things and stick to one thing or the other they end up liking. Okamoto-san has been living her life by this very principle.

When we meet her, she greets us. 'How's your day going?'
'It's okay,' we reply. 'Just a normal day.'
She then asks, 'Why just okay? Aren't you having a good day?'
'It's just an ordinary day—nothing special,' we respond.
She continues. 'How was your lunch? Did you enjoy it?'
We reply in the affirmative.

Finally, Okamoto-san smiles. 'If you had a good lunch, then why not be happy about it?'

She believes that finding happiness in small, everyday things is crucial. She wants everyone to find something that brings them joy and actively seeks happiness in everyday moments: no matter how small, even something as simple as enjoying a good lunch.

Despite long hours of sitting required for translation work, Okamoto-san maintains a balanced routine. She takes breaks in between to engage in activities like cooking, cleaning, and gardening. These tasks not only provide physical movement but also offer a change of scenery and a sense of accomplishment.

Recently, Okamoto-san has expanded her voluntary work to include spending time near a school. In Japan, it's possible to volunteer by simply keeping an eye on children as they head home from school. She does just that, watching over the kids as they make their way back, something she also enjoys. As they return, she also strikes up conversations with them, cherishing the joy that comes from interacting with the younger generation.

When we speak to her, she tells us she is writing the reply to a letter send by a little kid. While volunteering, she would always say, 'Be careful, cross well, and do well,' but the kid never responded. However, the previous day, the kid had given her a little letter, thanking her for being there and looking out for them every day. 'I want you to live longer and stay healthy,' the letter said.

Okamoto-san is happy and thus penning a response. She says she would give it to him along with a candy.

By giving, she feels that she receives even more in return. We ask her, 'Wouldn't you rather stay home, take a nap, or just relax?' She firmly shakes her head, pushing along her little support cart as she walks. 'No, no.'

'This gives me so much fulfilment. Life, for me, is about seeing these little kids and people around me and giving them all my love.'

Okamoto-san values the opportunity to learn from others, believing that every interaction holds the potential for new discoveries. Interacting with people is another aspect of her routine that she treasures. She wakes up at 6.00 a.m. and walks for twenty-five minutes to join a group of ladies at a nearby park for *taiso,* which is a Japanese exercise known for benefiting people of all ages and abilities by promoting physical and mental well-being.

Actually, this exercise can be simply done at home, but then she says that there are a lot of people at the park, and when she is with them, she feels nicer. Besides stretching and exercising, she engages in conversations, exchanging tips and experiences with her fellow park-goers. In fact, sometimes, she makes some pickle and brings it to share with others, who also get something in return, and this way, they look forward to meeting each other every single day.

She has been following this routine for the past ten years. Initially, she started because she felt that how she began her mornings mattered—otherwise, her body would become stiff.

However, she struggled with motivation. Some days she exercised, while other days she didn't. Then she realized, 'If I'm with people, I'll feel more motivated. I need to step out of the house.'

And so, for the last decade, that's exactly what she has been doing.

Okamoto-san also recognizes the value of pursuing activities, even if one is not initially skilled at them. She enjoys *etegami,* the Japanese postcard art. While she admits that she is not particularly skilled at it, she believes this lack of expertise is what makes her want to try more.

'Do you ever feel down?' we ask her. 'And if so, what do you do? And that what's your advice to people when they get old?'

'In our everyday lives, we have to find something that we can concentrate on. Or do something—something you can get lost, absorbed into,' she replies.

Okamoto-san has turned hundred, but if you meet her, you'd never guess it. Her energy, warmth, and curiosity make it feel like she has discovered the secret to a life well-lived. She doesn't think about age or milestones—she simply wakes up every day and does what brings her joy.

And that's exactly what she has been doing—day after day, year after year. Whether she's translating books, exchanging smiles with schoolchildren, or sharing pickles with friends at the park, she fills her days with purpose and connection. To her, happiness isn't something grand or extraordinary—it's in the little moments, the simple joys, and the people around her.

Prof. Hasegawa's Ikigai Expert Commentary

Okamoto-san began translating books into Braille at the age of sixty, a task that most people would find challenging to learn at that age.

I believe that when she was young, she always had the desire and curiosity to learn but never got the opportunity. It was only after her kids and grandkids grew up that she started doing things she couldn't do earlier. And now, nearly forty years later, she has translated close to 300 books.

She also volunteers to watch over the kids in her community as they walk to school. According to her, what goes around eventually comes back to her. She also believes she receives multifolds of what she actually gives. The joy she feels after connecting with people provides her another reason to get out of the house and be useful to them. And in between her translation and community volunteering work, she cooks, takes care of her garden, and keeps her house tidy.

When I think about Okamoto-san's life, I realize that the way time is experienced varies from person to person. For some people, days seem to fly by, while others feel like they seem to last forever. For someone like Okamoto-san, whose days are filled with her regular routine of translating, tending to her garden, cooking, cleaning, and watching over the neighbourhood kids on way to school, time might feel steady and predictable.

But even in this rhythm of a routine life, there are moments when time can feel a little different, isn't it? For instance, when she pauses between her tasks and notices something small but special—a flower blooming in her garden, or kids' laughter as they walk to school. These moments may seem mundane, yet they add something new to her day. It's in these brief, unexpected moments and experiences that life becomes that bit more colourful, and it's often these little surprises that make you feel alive.

Mihaly Csikszentmihalyi's concept of 'Flow' refers to the state of deep focus and enjoyment people experience when they are fully immersed in an activity.[23]

Even mundane activities, when performed with focus and engagement, can lead to this sense of flow. Csikszentmihalyi explains that even tasks like washing dishes or walking can become joyful when they are performed with full attention and engagement. The mundane becomes meaningful when individuals focus on the process, by creating a sense of achievement or satisfaction in otherwise repetitive tasks.

Rituals are another powerful mechanism through which predictability and mundanity can be linked to joy. Studies suggest that engaging in rituals, even simple or daily ones, provides comfort, promotes well-being, and can heighten the enjoyment of ordinary moments. In a study it was found that rituals can enhance people's experiences of everyday activities.[24]

Even the smallest, most mundane rituals, such as lighting a candle before eating dinner or having a morning stretch routine, create a sense of purpose and make ordinary tasks feel more significant.

Okamoto-san beautifully and seamlessly combines both concepts of 'flow' and 'rituals' as she goes about her everyday life. Her ability to focus effortlessly during her daily routines helps her discover tiny little sparks of joy and fulfilment in what may seem like mundane daily tasks or chores. Consciously slowing down can help you notice things that you otherwise miss—similar to what is zen practitioners do.

Heartfelt advice for you from Okamoto-san

If you keep telling yourself, 'I cannot do this,' or 'I cannot do that,' nothing will happen. You will be stuck. Instead, just try out something new and continue doing it till it automatically becomes the reason you keep improving.

We hope something in Okamoto-san's story spoke to you.

Now feels like a good moment to turn inward—and take the next step on your own Ikigai365 journey.

Close your eyes and take a deep breath, reflecting on the following questions before writing down the answers:

Is there anything you recently started that was outside your comfort zone? What were the challenges you faced?

_____

_____

_____

What are you passionate about but hesitate to act upon, because it is outside your comfort zone?

_____

_____

_____

If Okamoto-san can, so can you. Take that first step today!

Sidebar: Traditional Japanese Games

Globally, many older adults experience cognitive decline as they age, with symptoms such as taking longer to remember words or becoming forgetful. In Japan, memory improvement games are popular and practiced daily to enhance cognitive functions like memory, attention, and problem-solving skills. People of all ages enjoy these games to keep their minds sharp and potentially prevent cognitive decline. Japan's emphasis on lifelong learning and mental fitness contributes to the popularity of these games.[25]

Sudoku is a globally popular logic-based number puzzle, where players fill a 9*9 grid with digits from one to nine, ensuring each row, column, and 3*3 sub-grid contains each number once. It improves logical thinking and concentration.[26]

Kai-awase is a traditional Japanese shell-matching game from the Heian period (794–1185 CE). It involves finding pairs of clamshell halves decorated with intricate designs. The game requires keen observation and memory skills, as players remember the locations of previously revealed shells.

Interestingly, the 'gai' in Ikigai comes from 'kai' of Kai-awase, meaning shell and value, making Ikigai translate to 'value of life'. These traditional games, deeply embedded in Japanese culture, offer more than entertainment.

What is your go-to game or activity to keep your mind sharp and healthy?

Key quote

'I have no special talents; I am only passionately curious.'
—Albert Einstein

Making Life an 'Eternal Spring'

Meet Kamo-san! The person with an enduring vitality.

Life's secret mantra: Do things that make you feel happy and alive.

A week after meeting us, Kamo-san is talking about the prospects of farming in India.

While we've come to interview him for his Ikigai journey of over ninety-three years, his daughter tells us we might have triggered a new Ikigai for him: to come, live, and work setting up greenhouses for farming in India.

But let's start from the beginning.

Kamo-san is the inventor of the concept of Kachoen, a bird and flower sanctuary. It's an unusual yet obvious combination, as a beautiful green area with flowers located in a cool environment will attract birds naturally.

Kamo-san's trigger to come up with this concept was his childhood interest in birds. He had once discovered a baby owl in an injured state and slowly nursed it back to health. This was the beginning of his love affair with birds. With flowers, right from his early days at the family farm, he slowly honed his skills of growing Japanese Iris, continuing to research and investigate while being on the job.

What sets Kamo-san apart is his curiosity to learn and experiment. He has travelled all over the world, and particularly to the Netherlands, to study the greenhouse farming techniques. Today, he is a global authority on growing Japanese Iris, inventing more than hundred new varieties of it and of various other flowers.

Seeing is believing. A walk into Kachoen complex through the entrance booth, after crossing a narrow wooden door, transports you to a paradise of flowers, greens, ponds, and bird houses with lush mountains in the backdrop. Entering this one-hectare complex elevates one's senses and spirit, connecting to another world altogether.

Kamo-san, who grew up on this farmland, walks us into his residential chambers, where their family heritage home, with a history of over 500 years, is located. Walking around the place, one can feel the intergenerational aura and warmth of the family in their grandmother's pictures. He also shows us his grandma's temple and the family dining table of five, which has a fire pit in the middle with everyone's names inscribed in Kanji script on their side. This dining overlooks a Japanese moss garden, nestled amid a turquoise pond, with reflections of the afternoon sun filtering through the trees, weaving magical visuals. It's a postcard picture, the kind that gets captured in one's imagination.

Then, we walk to the well spread-out greenhouse to see the vast expansive varieties of trees and flowers growing there, along with an entire row of bird zoo.

A beautiful pair of orange parrots overhear our conversation with Kamo-san, his daughter, and his grandson over an iced coffee.

'You are from India, hmm . . .' Kamo-san absorbs with a pause. 'India is a beautiful country. In the 1940s, I have transited from there once, back when the plane landed in Calcutta [now Kolkata] to refuel. I was in India for only two hours, while transiting on my way to Amsterdam for my greenhouse research,' he says.

'A greenhouse needs a temperate climate and should be located at an ideal altitude of 2,000 to 3,000 meters above sea level. In India, you have many such places,' Kamo-san adds. Quietly googling his claim, we come up with a list of hundred such locations in each corner of India.

'Your country is located at the centre of the world, so it is well located from a logistical point of view. How long did it take you to reach Tokyo?'

Eight hours, we reply.

'See—you are equidistant from Japan and Europe, with access to North America. You have the location, the climate, and hardworking people with the required agrarian skills,' says the extremely well-studied man who has been to over a hundred countries.

'I took my last flight pre-Covid. I am still healthy, and would love to come to India for farming. In fact, I could live there. I wouldn't even mind if I die there.'

That's the passion and energy of the man!

We softly remind him that if he is tired, we could end the interview. But responding with a smile, he says, 'I'm enjoying this conversion and discovering something new. In fact, I'm energized—forget being tired.'

This is one of the seven Kachoen properties located across Japan, with the largest one in the Mount Fuji area.

Kamo-san's daughter tells us that people come from long distances to visit. Once, she recalls, a lady had come to see the flowers on a stretcher, as she could not walk. Seeing the flowers bloom in the glory of the sun and enjoying the chirping of the birds, she had said, 'I can now die in peace.'

'As a family, we opened up our home and garden to visitors several years ago, because we draw joy from their happiness,' her daughter adds. 'We had never planned for the Kachoen to be a touristic place; it just evolved that way as the word of this paradise of flowers and birds went around in the community. Soon, many people started flocking to see the never-seen-before varieties of Japanese Iris and enjoy the aura of this nature park.'

If you google Kamo-san, you may land upon Kimjongalia, a hybrid flower named after North Korea's Kim Jong II, for whom he innovated the variety.

But why for a dictator?

Surprised—being unaware of this Wikipedia post—he responds with a smile.'I get requests from different countries who want me to innovate flower species for them.' A similar one had come from North Korea. 'This one, then, became famous. You see, flowers have no country, and they love peace.'

He named this flower Kimjongalia because he couldn't think of another name. 'I'm no fan of Kim Jong II, nor am I judging him for who he was or his worldview,' he says.

And then, he calmly shifts the topic back to India. 'Trumpet Lily,' he says, pointing in its direction, 'is a plant that loves all kinds of climate, especially tropical settings. It is also very adaptable. I think it will be very happy in India.'

Surprised, we ask him about the Ikigai of plants. 'How do they think and feel?'

Kamo-san contemplates before answering. 'Yes, plants too have an Ikigai—it is flowering. This gives them a purpose, further serving the entire ecosystem consisting of bees, pollen, and other creatures. If plants did not have this purpose, they would have no reason to live,' he says. 'And making these plants flower is my Ikigai,' he adds.

Hearing his answer, we all look at each other and smile in amazement of the man's wisdom. Encouraged by his answer, we go on to further ask. 'What can humans learn from plants?'

A tough question, but he ponders for a while. 'There are things humans can learn from plants and there are things humans can't learn from plants,' he offers. 'Just like humans throughout history, plants also war with each other. They fight for soil, fertilizer, sunlight, and space, as they have the natural, human-like tendency to spread their specifics.'

But there is some variation. 'It's a little different from how humans battle, who can even fight for annihilation in extreme situations. For plants, it's merely a fight for survival,' he explains. 'There is a right place for the right plant, and once they find it, they feel happy and cease fighting.'

'When plants are happy, I am happy,' he adds. 'Helping them find their happy place is my Ikigai.'

What a beautiful notion, we think.

Kamo-san goes on. 'I feel grateful that my father, Tama-san, came up with this garden. As a child, it gave me a playground to experiment with new plants and flowers species each year. The idea just continued to grow, along with people's interest in it. This also encouraged us to create more Kachoen, bringing the technique of designing greenhouses and well-water irrigation without the use of electricity. This allows people to come to Kachoen and enjoy the flowers all-year around. This makes me happy.'

The point to note here is that Kamo-san's innovations are driven by his desire to give the visitors a year-round experience of flowers. 'What is most important to me is the feeling of being alive. I'm happy that I am alive and healthy, and I soon look forward to coming to India,' he says.

The story of Kamo-san is the story of eternal spring. But how does one live, so that life feels like an eternal spring? This is a point for many of us to ponder.

Can we create a 'stage of life' like the Kachoen—a beautiful home to birds and flowers that Kamo-san and his family have created and nurtured over decades?

Instead of following the patterns prescribed by the society, can we not learn from Kamo-san to set a 'stage of life', birthed from our deepest drivers—a space where we can do the things closest to our heart, and in the meantime, enrich the community and the ecosystem?

Prof. Hasegawa's Ikigai Expert Commentary

Kamo-san has been running this unique theme park for many years—it is all about connecting people with nature. Visitors come from all over to see his amazing exhibits filled with a variety of plants, beautiful flowers, and even birds. What is even more impressive is that the land that he has been working on has been in his family for nearly 400 years. Over the centuries, Kamo-san's ancestors have been passing down this land which he nurtures, breeding plants and caring for the birds. For him, this is more than just a park; it is also his family legacy.

Kamo-san believes that living things in nature, especially plants, have been around since the ancient times. They are still here with us today, and they will continue to exist long into the future. For example, a flower blooms in front of us—it starts as a seed, grows, blooms. And even after it withers, the seed remains, ready to bloom again when the time comes. Similarly, we all inherit many things—both tangible and intangible—from our ancestors. Hopefully, we want to and are able to pass them on to future generations that will come after us.

The Biophilia Hypothesis, proposed by Edward O. Wilson in 1984, suggests that we, humans, have an innate affinity for nature and its systems due to our evolutionary history. This subconscious connection contributes to emotional and psychological well-being. This can be seen in research evidence that exposure to green spaces can reduce stress, improve mood, and enhance cognitive functioning.[27]

Further, interaction with nature has also been linked to reduced symptoms of anxiety and depression.[28]

Also, experiencing awe in nature often inspires individuals to think beyond themselves, inspiring efforts to create lasting positive change.[29]

As you can see from these various facets, spending time with nature has many positive benefits that you can consider embracing and even passively enjoying from time to time. Kamo-san has dedicated his life to helping everyone access and enjoy nature in a variety of ways. One of his Ikigai triggers was when he, as a child, had found the fallen injured baby owl—another being his constant connection with plants. Seeing how happy people felt when they look at the plants likely makes Kamo-san feel really alive, fulfilled, and satisfied.

Each one of us can activate our own emotional well-being not just by being in nature, rather also by discovering ways to interact with it. What could be your trigger to experience nature in various ways, while being inspired to make life worth living every day?

Heartfelt advice for you from Kamo-san

Dedicate your life to something that intersects with nature and try and leave it in better shape than you find it, because you inherited it from previous generations, and it is your duty to pass it on to future generations.

Close your eyes and take a deep breath, reflecting on the following questions before writing down the answers:

Go find a physical object that best represents you. Describe why the object reflects you as a person.

_____

_____

_____

How do you feel connected to nature in your everyday life? What will you do to feel more connected to nature in future?

_____

_____

_____

You may wish to use the tool 'Connecting the Dots' in myIkigai365 nourishment journal.

If Kamo-san can, so can you. Take that first step today!

Sidebar: Kacho-en

In Japanese, *kacho* means 'flowers and birds,' and *en* means 'garden' or 'park.'

Together, *kacho-en* describes a 'flowers and birds park.' It is also a theme commonly found in traditional Japanese paintings featuring birds and flowers. Created during the Edo period (seventeenth to nineteenth centuries), these artworks beautifully blend birds and flowers. You can find kacho-en depicted in various Japanese art forms such as paintings, prints, ceramics, and textiles. Typically, it portrays birds in their natural surroundings, accompanied by a variety of flowers or plants. More than just visually pleasing, it is an important part of Japan's art history, reflecting a deep appreciation for nature and beauty.

Sidebar: Ikigai of Plants

Plants are super important for us humans, giving us things like food and clothes. But guess what? Plants kind of need us too. Talking nicely to them, giving them hugs or kisses actually helps them grow better. And did you know, spending time in forests, *shinrin yoku*, (the Japanese practice of forest bathing) is not just good for people, but it makes plants happy too? It reduces stress for us and helps plants grow healthier.

Moreover, plants make sounds and react to little vibrations—maybe it's their way of trying to talk to us. So, it turns out, plants and we are like buddies, helping each other out.

Cool, right?

Key quote

'Ask what makes you come alive, and go do it'.

—Howard Thurman

Craft A Beautiful Life . . .
One Day at a Time

Meet Miyauchi-san!

Life's secret mantra: The magic key to enjoyment and fulfilment is to completely immerse yourself and get absorbed in whatever you do. And do it regularly with discipline.

Miyauchi-san was born the eldest of six siblings into a lower middle-class family. Her father passed away early, so her mother went to work to help make ends meet. Soon, the burden of most household chores fell on the shoulders of a young Miyauchi-san, who was then in her teens. Needless to say, the family also couldn't afford to send her for higher studies.

As a young teenager, Miyauchi-san liked art and crafts and tried various small projects at home whenever she could find some free time. One day, when free classes started being offered at a nearby community centre, she wanted to use this opportunity to learn and improve her skills. But all those classes had already filled up, leaving her with the sole option of learning *shippoyaki*, the Japanese art of enamelware. So, she decided to pursue this. Soon, she not only became good at creating beautiful things, but ended up being her teacher's assistant.

Along the way, in her late-twenties, Miyauchi-san got married and had two daughters—all the while giving her best at taking care of the household and the family. She continued with her practice for a while but eventually got busy with children. Moreover, as shippoyaki also demands a special oven and some tools, which she couldn't afford to have at home, she decided to learn something new—something that could easily be done at home with young children around.

This was when she began learning mola patchwork quilting, a reverse appliqué technique, making different items like bags, brooches, and tapestries. Quickly, she mastered it—so much so, she not only started teaching others, but also began to sell them to her friends in the neighbourhood and local boutique shops for some extra income. Even today, after many decades, you can see amazing one-of-a-kind mola and shippoyaki artworks adorning her home.

Once her daughters grew up, got married, and moved out, she had so much more free time to teach. She also felt that she had the flexibility to learn a whole lot of things she did not know earlier or couldn't afford to—either due to time or money constraints.

Miyauchi-san's husband passed away when she was seventy, and suddenly, she felt couldn't cope with the loss. She felt miserable. In those moments of grief, she realized that she felt slightly better on days she tried to keep a routine. Thus, she decided to build one and get back to it every day. The more she kept up with her routine, the better she felt. So, while she initially struggled with living alone and experienced depression, she opted to keep herself busy, rediscovering her passion for art and handicrafts.

To cope with her solitude, Miyauchi-san began picking up new skills, and one day, while sitting alone, stumbled upon a unique art form. She started rolling and cutting old magazines, creating beautiful patterns. She segregated these rolled papers colour wise which became her new passion, and she spent her days making rolls of paper and exploring different ways to use them. As in the past, she even began teaching it to others, while participating in various art contests and winning awards in her eighties for her work.

Eventually, she found out she also wanted to explore ways to improve her fitness and posture, and hence, decided to sign-up for swimming lessons.

It has now been more than two decades since Miyauchi-san's husband passed away. Both her daughters are married and well-settled in Tokyo and visit her only once or twice a year. But she doesn't complain or resent their absence. Instead, she focuses on maintaining a routine that has both a daily rhythm and a weekly variety to it. Everything—grocery shopping, swimming, cooking, cleaning, meeting friends, craftwork, reading, journaling, watching TV—has its own time, and the days are fixed; it is tweaked as needed, of course. She insists that a routine is critical to get-going. Every single day, she also journals even the minutest of details of her daily routine.

Miyauchi-san wakes up at six every morning, and starts her day with stretches, before dedicating herself to cleaning the house and doing the laundry. She takes great care in preparing balanced meals for herself and avoids eating out.

Back at her house, she has created a quiet corner for herself. There, she sits with her morning cup of coffee, looks outside the window, reflects on the previous day, the weather, imagines how the day will turnout, and allows the outside views to dance with her mood.

Aside from her artistic pursuits, Miyauchi-san's commitment to self-care and maintaining a well-kept home is remarkable. Her house is beautifully maintained, reflecting her attention to cleanliness and organization. She has also maintained a regular swimming routine for the past twenty years, never skipping a day. She continues to learn and grow, attending cooking lessons, and exploring new crafts.

Despite the challenges of commuting, she takes two trains and a bus to reach her cooking class, where she learns to make sweets, also inviting her friends to enjoy them. When asked how long she plans to continue swimming and pursuing her lessons and crafts, Miyauchi-san confidently states that she will do so until the day she passes away.

Her zest for life and positive outlook are truly inspiring, as she embraces each day with enthusiasm and vibrancy.

Prof. Hasegawa's Ikigai Expert Commentary

Miyauchi-san spends her daily life not only creating art but also trying to be creative in other ordinary daily ways such as cooking. She spends her time in her own world—her living space is not closed off, but open to the outside world, extending from the inside to the outside.

From the outside, Miyauchi-san's life may appear to repeat the everyday monotony. But in her inner world, she spends her days with a curiosity to discover tiny differences. She finds extra ordinary things in the daily ordinary mundane tasks, finding joy and fulfilment in small discoveries.

The Creative Achievement Model (CAM), developed by Shelley Carson in 2012, bridges the gap between creative potential (the ability to generate ideas) and creative achievement (the tangible realization of those ideas). This model highlights the factors that enable individuals to transform creativity into measurable outcomes, providing a framework for understanding the psychology of creativity and completion.

In a nutshell, the Shelley model can be a good reference for your pursuit of creative achievement. It explores how cognitive traits, personality, motivation, skills, and environment influence an individual's ability to complete creative projects. Creative individuals also often rely on rituals and routines (for instance, daily writing schedules for authors) to create consistent opportunities for inspiration, while allowing flexibility within their creative work.[30]

Why don't you try to turn creating art into an enjoyable experience in your daily life?

Before starting, try to imagine what you will make, what preparation is required, and how you will piece together everything to create a new work of art. Just like Miyauchi-san, after collecting all the required material, jump right in, and begin to work on the specifics. Also, be prepared for things to not always go as you imagined them to. So, just like Miyauchi-san—flexibly but effortlessly—enjoy the revisions as you work towards completion.

Viewed through an Ikigai lens, creative activity combines two things: an imagined future of what a successfully completed project will look like, as well as a present enjoyment of the creation process. This iterative back-and-forth between the future and the present creates an infinite loop of *waku-waku*—Japanese for excitement or thrill. This keeps inspiring you towards continuous action without a feeling of a 'boring routine'.

Heartfelt advice for you from Miyauchi-san

Don't chase good health. Keep looking for things that you enjoy and feel satisfied doing them. You will automatically feel in good health and spirits.

We hope Miyauchi-san's story sparked a moment of reflection for you.

Consider this a gentle prompt to begin noticing your own Ikigai365 story as it unfolds, one step at a time.

Close your eyes and take a deep breath, reflecting on the following questions before writing down the answers:

What is your own 'personal sanctuary' for daily reflections?

_____

_____

_____

Where is it? What time of the day? Why do you look forward to it?

_____

_____

_____

You may wish to use the tool, 'Coffee Date with Yourself' in myIkigai365 nourishment journal.

If Miyauchi-san can, so can you. Take that first step today!

Sidebar: The Art of Life

How many people strive to create something valuable from nothing? What one sees as waste, another may find useful. It's all a matter of perspective.

Many artists, like Miyauchi-san, see value in things others discard. Influenced by the Japanese concept of *mottainai*, which translates to 'What a waste!' it expresses regret when something valuable is wasted, conveying appreciation for resources and a desire to use them fully. Mottainai is rooted in the four R's: reduce, reuse, recycle, and respect.

Interestingly, Arte Povera (meaning 'poor art'), the Italian art movement of the 1960s, also emphasized the use of simple, everyday materials. Artists used earth, rocks, paper, wood, cloth, and industrial materials like metal and glass to explore themes of nature, industrialization, and the human condition. They aimed to break down the boundaries between art and life, often focusing on the relationship between man and nature.

Concepts like Mottainai and Arte Povera remind us that with a shift in perspective, we can transform the ordinary into the extraordinary. Isn't it amazing?

Short Story

Preserving Memories, Not Counting Years

Meet Hakotani-san!

His story is one of resilience, determination, and a lifelong passion for learning.

Orphaned at a very young age, he was raised by his grandparents. Despite the hardships that came with losing his parents, he never allowed his circumstances to define him. Instead, he focused on his education, determined to carve out a better future for himself. A diligent student with a deep passion for history and literature, Hakotani-san stood out for his intellectual curiosity. His thirst for knowledge went beyond the classroom; he was always searching for ways to expand his understanding of the world. However, growing up during a time when access to information and the exchange of ideas was limited, Hakotani-san realized that knowledge had to be sought, not simply handed to him. In high school, this realization led him to create a journalism club—an endeavour that sparked what would become a lifelong career in journalism eventually.

Now ninety-two, what is most remarkable about Hakotani-san is how youthful he appears for his age. His posture is upright and strong, and he radiates vitality that defies the passing of time. His wife, Sayoko-san, shares this vitality; she, too, appears much younger than her years.

Their home, simple yet immaculate, reflects the care and attention they've maintained over the years without any outside help. Hakotani-san and Sayoko-san, high school sweethearts, later married and raised two daughters creating a home filled with love, understanding, and support. Their daughter fondly recalls the deep bond between her parents. 'I've never seen two people so in love with each other,' she says. 'And it's lasted this way for all these years.'

When asked about the secret to their long-lasting relationship, Sayoko-san offers wise words. 'Falling in love is easy, but staying in love takes work. You have to keep working at it, and you have to respect each other.' Their daughter adds, 'I've never once heard them speak ill or complain about each other and, for that matter, of anyone in all these years. They are always kind, patient, and full of respect for each other.'

In addition to his loving nature, sharp memory, and intellect are other defining traits. His ability to recall events with astonishing accuracy, right down to the exact date, has made him a family historian of sorts. His daughters and grandchildren frequently consult him to verify facts or help recall important events. The grandchildren even affectionately refer to him as their 'walking and talking encyclopedia'! They recall watching quiz shows together, where Hakotani-san would answer every question correctly before the contestants had a chance. And yet, despite his vast knowledge, he remains humble in demeanour.

What makes Hakotani-san's memory all the more impressive is that it doesn't come effortlessly. After retiring from his forty-years-long career in journalism, he noticed his memory was beginning to slow down. So, instead of resigning himself to this decline, he made a personal vow: He would do everything in his power to keep his mind sharp for as long as he lived. Then, in retirement, this commitment to mental acuity became his guiding principle.

Drawing on his deep love of history, Hakotani-san began immersing himself in historical research as a way to keep his mind active. But he didn't stop there. Understanding that one of the best ways to solidify knowledge is by teaching it to others, twenty-eight years ago, he founded a history club. Here, he gathers groups of people who share his passion for the past, and together, they visit historic sites, with Hakotani-san serving as their guide and storyteller. Each trip is a chance for him to share the significance of the places they visit, enriching both his own mind and his fellow travellers'. These excursions also serve another important purpose: They often involve long walks that keep him in excellent shape.

In addition to his mental exercises, Hakotani-san is meticulous about maintaining his physical health, ensuring that his body remains as healthy as his mind. He follows a well-balanced, nutrient-rich diet, and avoids processed foods. His daily routine is as disciplined as ever—he wakes up early, completes his morning rituals, and always changes into clothes ready for the day. To support his hips and to maintain his posture, he wears a belt. In fact, he seems prepared to head out at any moment—rain or shine. This attention to detail in his routine plays a crucial role in his vitality.

Another aspect of Hakotani-san's remarkable life is his physical agility, and the reflex so sharp that he continues driving until now. Every week, he makes a trip to the local library, where he borrows four to five books spanning various genres. With a reading pace of over 200 books a year, his thirst for knowledge shows no sign of slowing down. What's even more impressive is that he retains almost everything he reads, an ability that continues to amaze those around him. He enjoys playing shogi with friends, taking five-kilometre-long walks daily, and cherishing time with his grandchildren and great-grandchildren.

'People often focus on working out to build muscles,' he says, 'but they don't give as much attention to their brains. The brain is just like a muscle—the more you use it, the stronger it gets.'

Hakotani-san insists on finding something you love that moves your body. 'For example, borrow books on your favourite topics from the library, which gives you an opportunity to go out to borrow and return books,' he explains. 'When something piques your interest, you'll want to visit related places and take action—it's natural and not forced.'

Hakotani-san's life is a shining reminder that it's never too late to make positive changes and that staying engaged with the world is key to a fulfilling, active life. His unwavering commitment to learning, his disciplined routine, and his genuine interest in the world around him prove that age is just a number. With the right attitude, anyone can live a vibrant, intellectually rich life, even into their golden years.

Short Story

Authenticity Breeds
Resilience in Service

Meet Tadao-san!

Tadao Yasuoka, an eighty-three-year-old retiree in Kyoto, defies the common narrative of post-retirement idleness. He managed his construction business until retiring eight years ago, and since, he has embraced gardening as a newfound hobby, despite having no prior experience or knowledge of it. 'One can develop new hobbies at any stage of their life and must persist in trying new things,' he explains is his belief.

A cancer survivor, Tadao-san maintains a rigorous routine, waking up at 5.00 a.m. each morning for stretches and a brisk walk.

His destination?

His wife's cemetery, behind the neighbourhood shrine where he tenderly cares for the plants he's grown. She held a deep affection for flowers, particularly hydrangeas, and losing her ten years ago left a profound void. As a tribute to his late wife, he took it upon himself to plant numerous hydrangeas in the barren land surrounding the shrine. His efforts have, over time, turned the cemetery into a summer attraction, drawing visitors who admire the blossoms. 'My wife would be happy looking at the flowers around her,' he says with a gentle smile, eyes reflecting love and devotion.

Tadao-san believes that being active in the morning sets the tone for the entire day and provides him the right energy and inspiration. His is guided by the principles of *magokoro*, a Japanese term that means sincerity, deep appreciation, and heartfelt connection. He emphasizes the importance of genuine interactions undertaken by treating everyone with love and respect, regardless of their actions towards you.

He dislikes the Japanese term *kotonokare shugi*, a mindset of maintaining the status quo to avoid conflict. Tadao-san believes in actively addressing problems rather than remaining silent. He believes in confronting issues head-on, taking action and finding solutions, and his actions speak louder than words.

Living beside a picturesque green mountain, Tadao-san encountered a landslide during a typhoon, leaving a portion of the mountain barren. Taking matters into his own hands, he levelled the soil and planted various flowering trees and herbs, gradually transforming the area into a pleasant space. Now, local residents visit to relax and access the herbs grown there, while the school children come to learn about the plants. His innovative spirit didn't stop there. Recognizing the lack of greenery in winter, he creatively illuminated the area using lights from his home, adding more year after year.

He even built a shed nearby with tools from his construction days, so people could borrow them for gardening, DIY projects, or for anything else they needed. The shed helps in fostering a sense of community where neighbours discuss their projects and help each other out. He figured everyone could use a helping hand sometimes.

Tadao-san's impact extends beyond his garden. He noticed the challenges faced by elderly residents without cars, who couldn't easily access the train station due to steep roads in the neighbourhood. Through tireless efforts, he petitioned and collaborated with local authorities, to secure a free, regular-interval mini-shuttle bus for the community, complete with benches, and a vending machine.

Additionally, on one of the bus stops, he constructed a small altar with a coin box for offerings, encouraging people to use the coins to enjoy a cup of coffee or a drink while waiting for the bus.

His mantra to get things done? 'Effort, effort, and more effort.' His dedication to his community earned him recognition, receiving a 'Good Citizen Award' from the Kyoto prefecture. Despite his accolades, Tadao-san remains grounded, and constantly seeks opportunities to improve the lives of those around him, treating everyone with respect regardless of age or social standing. Another virtue he cherishes is being genuine.

He dislikes *mikakedaoshi*, the act of appearing good superficially, lacking substance or ability. He emphasizes the importance of looking beyond appearances and focusing on who people truly are. Tadao-san also dislikes the term *jijikusai*, which refers to outdated ideologies. He believes in progressive thinking and adapting modern perspectives and persistence in problem-solving.

Despite losing his father at a young age and encountering life's inevitable ups and downs, Tadao-san embodies resilience. When asked about overcoming adversity, he offers a profound insight. 'When I stumble, I take it as a sign from God to change direction.' Even with his cancer returning, Tadao-san continues to live life to the fullest. He acknowledges the days when he feels physically and mentally drained by treatment, but he doesn't let it hold him back. His approach to bouncing back is both simple and inspiring. 'The best way is to change my environment. Sometimes, it's a walk in nature, a meal with friends, a drive or even a karaoke session. If I can't go out, I focus on the future: planning for next season's plantings, festive Christmas lighting, or simply something fun to look forward to. It's all about shifting my focus and staying positive.'

What is Tadao-san's final piece of advice?

'Irrespective of your age, never forget to have fun and enjoy life. Follow your interests and try out as many new hobbies or experiences as you can and do everything whole heartedly, and there will never be a dull moment in your life.'

In a world where many elderly individuals struggle with idleness, Tadao-san stands out, advocating for the importance of developing new interests regardless of age. His story reminds us that resilience isn't just about weathering storms, but also about finding joy in the journey.

Now that you've finished reading all the stories in the 'Winter' chapter, we invite you to take a quiet moment to try the Ikigai365 Reflection > Action Tool below. It's a gentle way to help you stay connected to your own sources and feelings of Ikigai.

Ikigai365 Reflections > Action Tool

(This exercise takes approximately 60 minutes or longer to complete)
(Recommended frequency: Anytime you feel the need to step back/reflect/get a boost)

Here and Now
Present feelings or emotions
you are experiencing

Past memories
or experiences
triggered

Future
hopes or dreams
rekindled

What change
do you
choose to make

Now, what is the one action you will take today or start tomorrow ?

I will

Epilogue

Which story inspired you the most? Who resonated with you the best?

Close your eyes. Take a deep breath. Tick only one story from each:

- Fujio-san: Life Worth ≠ Net Worth
- Hamano-san: Connections That Celebrate Generations
- Koko-san: Feeling Alive Here-And-Now = Life Without Regrets
- Yumi-san: True Caring = Guilt-free Self-Care
- Natsu-san: Building Happier Workplaces
- Kato-san: Caring is the Ultimate Form of Giving
- Midori-san: Smile of Gratitude Lights Up The Heart
- Hanazawa-san: Creating my Own *Ibasho*—A Place to Belong
- Sumida-san: Balance Impact with Connection
- Miho-san: Strength + Beauty = Self-Worth
- Masako-san: Life Becomes Worthy When You Start 'Living It'
- Ishizaki-san: Re-Wire.. Don't Retire
- Kaizuka family: Somehow… It All Works Out

- Teraguchi-san: My Life. My Pace. My Stage.
                          My Sanctuary
- Yano-san: Fragility of Life Fuels
                          Spirit of Innovation
- Megumi-san: Kimono-inspired Vitality
- Yasuo-san: Learning ∞ Sharing Cycle Drives
                          Youthfulness
- Ogawa-san: Curiosity is Ageless
- Okamoto-san: Giving Feels Like Receiving
- Kamo-san: Making Life an Eternal Spring
- Miyauchi-san: Craft a Beautiful Life, One
                          Day at a Time
- Hakotani-san: Preserving Memories, Not
                          Counting Years
- Yasuoka-san: Authenticity Breeds Resilience
                          in Service

Why did these stories resonate? Most likely, they may have awakened some of your own Ikigai seeds and helped you tune in to your own Ikigai sources. Somewhere, they might have even stirred up something in your past–present–future. They might have also helped you tune-in to your emotions and put a finger on what makes you feel alive or what makes you feel fulfilled.

Thank you for joining us on this exploration of authentic Japanese Ikigai, the way everyday Japanese people live their Ikigai journeys. We hope the stories and personal reflections have sparked a flame of curiosity and to continue on your own Ikigai journey of self-discovery.

Across all these stories, you would have seen that the sky is never pristine blue. Rather, there are clouds always—often dark, with thunderstorms. Just like everyone's life has ups and downs, authentic Ikigai journeys will feel like a roller-coaster when you truly tune in to all the emotions, both positive and negative.

While reading about the lives of these amazing people, you might have seen glimpses of your own hopes and aspirations or regrets and pains. The beauty of Ikigai lies not only in the stories shared. but in the resonance it creates with your own experiences.

Prof. Hasegawa believes that just like there are three primary colours—red, blue, and yellow—every other colour is a composite of these, mixed with black and white. Paul Ekman identified six basic emotions: anger, disgust, happiness, sadness, fear, and surprise.[31] We can see these as elements and combine each of them to complex emotions.

Every other emotion we feel is a composite of these primary emotions experienced though the past-present-future lens of our own unique lives. But our upbringing (education and social norms) doesn't necessarily train us to process these emotions or encourage us to express them, and often, we grow up numbing them out—especially the negative ones. These hamper our ability to, one, embrace whole-heartedly the daily roller-coaster of emotions we need to feel human; and two, connect these emotions to the source triggers of events—both in present life and/or past–future thoughts.

Ikigai365 is a small stepping stone to unpacking these on your own. The myIkigai365 Nourishment Journal in Part 2 of this book provides you with the tools to get started. Prof. Hasegawa's work has also highlighted that self is the only agent of change for feeling good about oneself. He equates feeling alive with making others happy/serving others as feeling fulfilled.

We sincerely hope that this book has fulfilled its purpose, as stated at the beginning, to share the authentic Japanese perspective on Ikigai—how the people of Japan perceive and experience their Ikigai and how they embark on their own unique Ikigai journeys, making every day worth living. Ikigai is not something to chase; rather, it is something you feel every single day.

As we conclude this adventure, remember that this book is not a mere read-and-forget experience; it's an ongoing dialogue with your own life. Embrace it as a life's journal, a companion on your journey toward understanding what truly makes you come alive and feeling fulfilled. It's small enough to fit in your bag, so take it along, especially on your nature trips or holiday breaks.

When you set aside time for yourself to reflect on where you are and where you want to go, consider bringing this book along. Picture yourself in your favourite café, sipping a latte, or relaxing in a park under a cherry tree, a gentle breeze brushing by as you flip through the pages. You might find yourself reading your handwritten notes from years ago, checking in on how you've grown as a person. We hope this book can accompany you on your journey through life's ups and downs, and if it helps you in any way, our purpose will be fulfilled.

In closing, we extend our deepest gratitude for allowing us to be part of your Ikigai exploration. May your days be filled with purpose, feeling alive and fulfilled as you spend each breath. As you continue your journey, remember that the adventure of Ikigai is not a destination but a lifelong quest to find meaning in every step.

May your Ikigai365 journey continue, and we wish you all the best in your daily rollercoaster of feeling alive, feeling fulfilled, and tuning into new sources of Ikigai!

We leave you with a beautiful Japanese quote: 桜梅桃李, or *obaidori*, which means, 'the flowers of cherry blossoms/plum blossoms/peach blossoms/apricot blossoms all look very similar, and bloom in spring. Yet they don't compete to bloom ahead of one another.'

Likewise, while all of us are equal as human beings, we all have our own individual beauty, and our own time and way to blossom. There is no need to compare or compete with others.

We hope you embrace your Ikigai365 journeys at mypace!

As we bid you sayonara, and leave you to move forward on your own Ikigai journey, we thought you might be wondering what motivated Prof. Hasegawa to dedicate his life to Ikigai research in Japan.

While there were a variety of experiences that kept sparking his interest and kept him occupied over the decades, a recurring nostalgia was a song from his junior high school days: 'Shujinkou' by Masashi Sada. It seemed to have left a deep impression on a young Prof. Hasegawa that continued to inspire him as he developed his expertise in the field of Ikigai.

The soulful song meanders effortlessly between the past, present, and future, weaving in both the physical and emotional that inundates all our lives. The song's ending pretty much sums up the one feeling of Ikigai we want to leave you with: You are the agent in control of your Ikigai journey, and that you hold the pen that will write the story of your life going forward.

Why We Wrote This Book

Hasegawa-sensei

I finished my research on Ikigai in 2003. On that day, I was also turning thirty-years-old, had earned my doctoral degree at the graduate school, was planning to pursue Clinical Psychology research, and practice as my primary focus.

However, I was still regularly writing overview papers on Ikigai.

In 2017, I received an inquiry from abroad about Ikigai, and initially, I didn't understand the world taking interest in it. The next thing I knew, I had understood the situation and learned that Ikigai was attracting attention abroad. However, I felt that this widely popular Ikigai model was a little different from the authentic Japanese sense, in particular, the connection between earning money and Ikigai—that is Hatarakigai, or work worth doing.[32] This is why I decided to get involved in research on Ikigai again.

After talking to Shiv, who is from India but lives in Singapore, and Rajiv, who lives in India, as well as their colleagues Sumathy and Rati, the idea of writing a book on this subject came to fruition. Nick from Melbourne, who although is not a co-author of the book, also encouraged me.

Looking back, I had already planned to write a doctoral dissertation on Ikigai and how it evolves through one's life in my late-twenties—something even my advisor, Dr Tanji Hoshi, mentioned to me. While I had stopped my research, this time, with the help of my collaborators, I was able to collect data and address the issue of lifelong fulfilment of purpose in life. I am also very pleased to be able to introduce the Ikigai Programme, which incorporates the techniques of clinical psychology, my field of specialty.

On a lighter note, working on this book has given me an opportunity to travel abroad.

Sumathy-san

I wanted to share my journey that has been over twenty-five years in the making. I've been lucky enough to spend all this time in Japan, diving headfirst into the culture and language. It's been quite a ride, and along the way, I stumbled upon something truly fascinating: the concept of Ikigai. This was long before it became a global trend. I saw how it works wonders in the lives of everyday Japanese people, helping them lead lives full of purpose, in their own unique way. This was way before it became it had become a big global trend.

One thing that had really struck me was the incredible spirit of the elderly there. They are full of life, energy, and stories that could light up a room. It got me thinking, especially now that the world is looking for ways to live better and live longer. It's become my dream to share all that I've seen and felt with others.

As I started sharing these stories with my close friends and family, something amazing happened: I noticed positive changes happening in their lives too. And it hit me again—we get inspired by people who are just like us, people we see every day, not just celebrities on screens. It's like a spark that makes us think, 'Hey, if they can do it, so can I.'

We all play different roles, right? Daughter, mother, sister, friend—you name it. And what I've found is that having role models for each of these can be a game-changer. Whenever I'm faced with a tough or uncertain situation, I ask myself: What would my role model do? It's surprising how much clarity and motivation this question brings. I sincerely hope that you'll find your role model in one of the stories here.

Collecting these stories and observing these people have had such a profound impact on me. This journey has taught me so much: It has opened up my heart to empathy, made me less judgmental, and more accepting of people as they are. It's given me the nudge to try new things, connect with people, and the biggest one being the realization that age is just a number.

This book is my way of sharing all of this with you. These stories are like gems that I want you to discover as well, because sometimes, just by observing, you can make a positive shift in your own life. It's about finding those sparks that ignite something in you and realizing that you've got it all within you to be able to lead a fulfilling life.

Rajiv-san

For me, Ikigai is a process of understanding the process of life. How do we live? How should we live? How could we live better?

When I started this journey over fifteen years ago, I didn't know that I would get the privilege to work with the finest minds in this space and co-author a book together.

Moreover, the journey and the process of writing this book has deepened and clarified my own understanding of Ikigai. As they say in Hindi, it's *paisa vasool* for me—I have got my money's worth. For me, my time is the only true wealth I have.

Each minute with this bunch—with all our debates and differences—make me ponder and discover another facet of Ikigai. It's like the unfurling of a petal.

I had gone to Japan with a notion that Ikigai is the purpose of life. But that is only a statement. It's hard to intuitively relate real-life situations with it. When I came back, I had understood that Ikigai is the feeling of being alive, in that moment, when life touches you in a way, a moment that just takes your breath away. One recalls such moments vividly: the birth of our children, or when our elder parents held our hand and shared the deepest feeling. It could also be using time in a way it makes one feel alive and life worth living, lifting away dark clouds for just that moment.

This process of understanding life, what makes it worth living, and striving to make the most of it, is the reason I wrote this book. Believe you me, several moments of this journey of writing this book have triggered my own Ikigai.

It would be a matter of great joy for me when this book brings an impact in the form of readers' understanding of their own Ikigai and improves their life's worth.

We would want to interact with our readers and be able to know their stories to be able to further learn from it and deepen our understanding of Ikigai.

My Ikigai is to help people discover their Ikigai. I use this process in my business, my family, my friends, and with anyone who gives me an opportunity to connect with their lives as a coach or otherwise.

I love deep research on topics of interest to me. The process of writing the book has made us debate, authenticate, and rationalize our thought processes. The stories of Ikigai journeys in this book and the application of our existing tools developed on their lives will help the readers understand Ikigai in a more relatable way. It has been a ravishing process, and there were several moments along with way that, as a team, took our breath away.

Speaking of the team, I'm someone who loves shared growth journeys. This joy of sharing is much more precious to me than the joy of having, hence I could say I am a team person first.

Navigating the challenges of working in a diverse team was something I relished. And while I have been leading teams in my business for years, working in this one was a truly refreshing experience.

This book has given me an opportunity to work with gurus like Hasegawa-san, a master Ikigai researcher and professor, whom I first met at a Tokyo hotel in 2019. It was him who further introduced me to Shiv—a not-so-easy-to-please student of life. While Shiv has transformed his life from a multinational company honcho to a self-paced life coach and professor, he retains his MNC process rigour into everything he does.

Sumathy, whom I met through Shiv, shared a common passion for connecting with people deeply and learning from their lives—as was assured to me by Shiv, and correctly so. The journeys we have taken together to meet people and collect their Ikigai journeys featured in this book are all Sumathy's handiwork. She truly knows to link in and find the right people to be featured in the book. The diversity of stories, from age twenty-eight to over a hundred, ranging from blessed coffee man to gut health transformer to old age worker, have happened because of her.

Rati and I have worked together for over thirteen years, and it has been amazing to see this relationship evolve from that of a subordinate, to a colleague, and to a friend—all the while retaining her original touch of being our class monitor and holding all of us accountable with her astute project management of the book journey.

In summer of 2023, Hasegawa-san gifted us a Japanese book on clinical psychology he had co-authored. I couldn't do much beyond appreciating its aesthetics and the intent with which he had gifted it to us. During our chats with him, I realized this is the eleventh book he has written. I was amazed by the simplicity and humility of the man, who is so calm, and frets and fumes only when we are running 120 seconds behind schedule for an interview or lunch!

Had this book not been written, I would have never got ten to work with this multi-national, multi-cultural team. The experience has quenched my thirst for learning, which is also a key Ikigai building block for me.

Harmonious working of a team and leveraging everyone's unique gift is Ikigai, and this teamwork triggered my Ikigai of joy of researching, co-creating and sharing.

Shiv-san

About five years ago, when I made a career switch and took a sabbatical, I had encountered a lot of new experiences and stimuli. You could say I was both lost and felt a vacuum, because for decades, my work and career had become one of the dominant sources of Ikigai in my adult life. Suddenly, what appeared to the outside world as a well-thought decision that garnered reactions such as brave and lucky—far from my former day-to-day life.

Despite living in Japan for nearly a decade in my early career, I hadn't really heard of the term Ikigai until 2019, when someone showed me the famous four-circled diagram. My gut reaction was that it didn't feel like Ikigai. This prompted me to research more, eventually leading me to meeting Hasegawa-sensei, who had conducted decades of extensive research on this subject. We connected instantly, and through our discussions, I felt inspired to deepen my understanding of Ikigai—all rooted in Hasegawa's lifework. The reason I felt inspired to write this book was to contribute in an ever-so small way, to enable people to take charge of improving their own lives, to create an ever-growing and evolving community of Ikigai365 practitioners that support self-awareness and self-care in a real-life way, full of ups and downs.

This is also my way of acting on a few things that trouble me as a person. At a macro level, the world continues to become increasingly divisive and polarized. As someone who values unity over division—possibly because of my formative decade of professional adult life in Japan, where harmony was a core value—I genuinely and unwaveringly believe that every human being is equal. However, we all take wildly different paths, experiences, and opportunities—somewhere along the way into adulthood, these get calcified into labels, norms, and attitudes, which get further complicated by every deafening noise around us.

When Hasegawa once said that one of his life's mission was to help put the 'being' back in 'human being', it was an 'aha!' moment which made me realize that in today's fast-paced, continuously-changing, left-brained, science and logic-driven, money-oriented world, we have all evolved into 'human doings', and that we seem to be losing the art of both just 'being' and authentically connecting with how we are feeling.

At a micro level, everyone is increasingly—and rightly so—concerned about the ever-increasing tide of the mental health and loneliness epidemics we're staring at, with high levels of stress, anxiety, and depression. While working with a founder of a medical technology startup focused on helping stroke patients recover after traditional treatments had failed to move the needle, I was inspired by his paradigm and approach.

His view is that issues like mental health and lifestyle diseases don't start with germs, and hence, they cannot be solved solely through chemistry and chemicals. We need a different approach that helps humans heal themselves and experience life to the fullest. Of course, while Ikigai is not meant to be a substitute for clinical care provided by psychologists and other health professionals, it is a complimentary way that I hope will help more and more people around the world, while leading more alive and fulfilling lives in their own unique way every day.

Rati-san

Six years back, when I began digging into Ikigai, Rajiv spoke to me about his quest for exploring more about well-being and healthy longevity. Since then, there's been no looking back.

Without me even realizing, this project turned into something I'm really passionate about. To be honest, I didn't notice it at first, but soon enough, I found myself talking about it all the time. I'd discuss it with my family, friends, coworkers, and even people I just met at social gatherings. It slowly hit me that I couldn't help but chat about Ikigai. It's like I have entered this zone where I can't stop, and time flies by without me noticing.

Covid-19 was a tough time for all of us. For me, though, it became a turning point. It helped me make the final decision to start my own personal journey, following my true passion, my Ikigai. Concurrently, my voyage into motherhood during this phase brought about a significant transformation. I realized that being a mom is both amazing and really hard at the same time. Dealing with my energetic little one, I ended up forgetting to take care of myself. This made me understand how important it is to look after my own emotional and physical well-being, before even trying to help others.

Back in March 2020, right in the middle of the pandemic, I made a choice. I signed up with Institute for Integrative Nutrition (IIN) because I wanted to work on my overall health and well-being. Looking back, the past five years have been truly remarkable in terms of how I've changed personally. I discovered that taking care of yourself isn't only about the food you eat; it's also about nurturing different parts of your life that aren't related to food, like your life's purpose, sleep, and relationships etc.

Now, in 2024, I find myself working closely with the Ikigai365 team to co-author this book. Our goal is to inspire individuals through authentic Japanese Ikigai stories and support them in embarking on their own path of self-discovery to find their Ikigai.

Being involved in the creation of this book has truly been a highlight of my life. It's brought me numerous advantages and benefits.

I'm not only fortunate to connect and learn directly from the globally acclaimed Ikigai researcher, Prof. Hasegawa, who has authored multiple research papers on the topic, but also from Shivendu, an accomplished business expert and educator with extensive cross-cultural exposure, as well as Sumathy, who has spent over twenty-five years in Japan and embraced the language and culture profoundly. Furthermore, I am privileged to be under the guidance and mentorship of Rajiv, who has played an essential and fundamental role in shaping both my professional and personal journey over the course of the past thirteen years.

Working on this book had allowed me to share the knowledge and experiences I've gained on this journey. As time passes, I realize that I'm growing as a person. This project gave me a reason to travel alone, and through that, I discovered the importance of spending quality time with oneself. Travel enables this self-reflection.

I vividly recall my first field trip to Japan in June 2023. On the first day, I felt very upset and questioned whether I had made the right decision by leaving my six-year-old at home for the first time. However, by the second day, I began to feel better. I was experiencing the joy of spending time with myself for the first time. It wasn't just me who noticed the change; when I returned from Japan, I gradually became a better daughter, wife, and mother. My attitude towards everything changed—I was calmer and more at peace with myself. My husband even asked if I was the same person who had gone to Japan! He wants me to travel alone every few months, because he sees a better version of me whenever I return.

Now, I wake up every day with a sense of purpose, do my best in everything I do, and feel really good about what I've accomplished when I go to bed at night. Above all, work doesn't seem like work anymore!

Why We Wrote This Book
Together As a Team

Team Ikigai365 really shows what happens when you mix diverse backgrounds and experiences.

With Prof. Akihiro Hasegawa and Sumathy from Japan, Shivendu from Singapore, and Rajiv and Rati from India, our crew brought a unique blend to the table. Our work on this book is proof of the magic that happens when different cultures join forces for a shared goal!

This brings up an interesting question: Why and how have individuals from such varied backgrounds come together to co-author this book?

Let's hear the story!

Rati-san: Even though we come from different backgrounds, we're all united by a common mission. It feels like destiny brought each of us here—a bunch of unexpected twists led us to this collaboration. We all have our own reasons for being part of this book, but what really brings us together is our shared passion for spreading authentic knowledge about Japanese Ikigai.

Rajiv-san: I've known Rati for over a decade now, and we've worked on all sorts of projects together. My love for Ikigai got me digging deeper into the topic, and that's when I asked her to join me. We ended up connecting with Prof. Hasegawa, whom I met in Japan during the Cherry Blossom season in 2019. Japan was buzzing with colour and energy back then, and so was our exchange of ideas. Prof. Hasegawa, who's one of the kindest people I know, shared his years of Ikigai research with me—most of it in Japanese. At the time, he was at Toyo Eiwa University and travelled quite a distance to meet me. When I asked why he came all that way, he said he could sense my deep interest in Ikigai from my email, and that gave him the motivation to make the trip.

Hasegawa-sensei: Interestingly, around that time, Shiv, who was in Singapore and on his own Ikigai journey, reached out to me. Our shared passion led us to team up on creating content, tools, and workshops to spread a true understanding of Ikigai. We were supposed to meet face to face in early 2020, but then Covid happened, so we kept sharing ideas remotely. Then it hit me—why not introduce Rajiv to Shivendu and see what we could create together?

And let me tell you, that was just the beginning.

Shiv-san: Then, I pulled in my friend Sumathy, whom I have known for almost twenty years. She is amazing at building lasting relationships, and we fondly call her the 'Christopher Columbus' of our team, as she's always on the lookout for more stories to add to the book.

Sumathy-san: Ever since I shifted to Japan after getting married almost twenty-five years ago, I was always intrigued by the way Japanese people, especially the elderly, live a fulfilling life on their own terms. It's has been my dream to share what I have witnessed over the years. This is why, towards the end of year 2022, we collectively decided to co-create and work on this Ikigai book with the aim of making a global impact.

Rajiv-san: Honestly, initially, I didn't believe that we would be able to sustain the energy to keep going, as often, somewhere the initial excitement ways off. But I feel surprised that we have gone on to complete this book.

Sumathy-san: I believe the team's first field trip to Japan in June 2023 was a significant milestone, as it marked the first time we were all together under the same roof. It felt like a dream come true, putting human touch to faces on Zoom, as if we were indeed destined to meet and collaborate on this project. That's when the real bonding started.

Shiv-san: Over a lot of wine, beers, coffee, kombuchas the bonding continued . . .

Rati-san: Initially, there was a visible stress, a clash of ideas, and our understanding of Ikigai—particularly between Ikigai and Hatarakigai. The Ikigai365 presentation had started with a cross on the Venn diagram, at which Rajiv took a deep breath upon seeing. He was just trying to find words to express that we don't remove it, but instead, sort of put a question mark. It took us months to come to this conclusion that this was the way to put it out, and now, we are able to laugh at it.

Sumathy-san: I must add to that there were moments of tension and disagreement during the writing process, but these conflicts often led to new insights and solutions, ultimately enriching our understanding of Ikigai and contributing to the creation of this book.

Shiv-san: It is our common purpose, a common mission that everybody on this planet should live a life of Ikigai.

Rajiv-san: We see this book as just the beginning of this journey. We visualize a training and education business, where we put these tools up for people to start their journey towards their Ikigai.

Hasegawa-sensei: I believe that our journey together demonstrates the power of collaboration across cultures, and the magic that happens when people unite around a common purpose.

As we continue to explore and share the principles of Ikigai, our hope is that this book will inspire readers around the world to embark on their own paths, towards a meaningful and fulfilling life, with more and more reasons for feeling alive.

Part 2

myIkigai365 Nourishment Journal

myIkigai365 Nourishment Journal

This is ....'s personal toolkit for journeys of daily reflection and action!

We, at Ikigai365, hold a deep unwavering belief that a variety of regular guided reflections (some daily, some weekly, some monthly, and some ad-hoc) are key triggers/nudges for the self-as-agent to drive action to make regular progress on individual myIkigai365 journeys.

This Nourishment Journal is your *ibasho*—personal safe sanctuary—to create the space for you to get into your own myPace groove.

myPace is a unique Japanese term that combines the following essence:

> My own pace with + prioritizing myself from time to time
> (as it is good for me) + going at my own rhythm and flow,
> without external pressures.

This nourishment journal offers a set of tools best utilized as part of your daily and weekly routine—near your bedside table (not coffee table) as it's a deeply personal space that needs to be free from any extrinsic pressures, be it real or perceived. For instance, 'What will they say/think/feel if they see this?'

Each tool has a recommended frequency of practice and an expected time-taken-to-complete-with-quality to guide your planning.

(You can use the 'Coffee With Myself' tool to get into the virtuous cycle of making this a habit)

'Where awareness goes, energy flows' is a simple but powerful phrase that fits here, and will support your Ikigai365 journey. It is coined by Sivaya Subramuniyaswami, monk Dandapani's guru.

Think of your daily quest as a continuous infinite loop—on one side of the loop you are tuning-in to the seeds and triggers that are omnipresent, both in and around you.

On the other side of the loop is a roller-coaster of both positive and negative feelings that are triggered multiple times through every single day. Consciously connecting these triggers and feelings at myPace will help you identify and prioritize time spent with your own sources of Ikigai, all the while managing the triggers of the negative emotions that often come with your daily activities constrained by your roles associated with fulfilling familial duties, social commitments, and/or earning a livelihood. Our goal is to provide tools that help you build self-awareness and direct your energy toward what truly matters to you.

(You can deep dive more on this in the Ikigai > Hatarakigai tool in this journal)

Ikigai is not a process of discovery, rather a regular practice of trying to connect your triggers (sources of feeling alive and fulfilled) with your emotions (both positive and negative feelings).

This is an everyday journey of noticing and tuning-in to the seeds for these sources and feelings that exist all around you. To put it in Hasegawa-sensei's words, your Ikigai is already here. We, at Ikigai365, are just trying to help you tune in to it every day. Your Ikigai journey will help you slowly but surely shift from 'doing' into 'being'.

As a group of Ikigai practitioners, we have carefully crafted and curated these tools with dedication and passion. To inspire the 'present self-as-agent' inside you for taking action on your own Ikigai journey, we have tried and tested these tools across our Ikigai365 workshops to make sure they are simple, practical, intuitive, and impactful.

We hope you will definitely spare just a few minutes today, to at least try out 'What Makes Your Heart Smile' or 'Coffee Date with Yourself', so you start your 'myPACE Nourishment'.

If you are looking to take a break from your busy schedule and can spare twenty to thirty minutes, why not try out 'Ikigai365 Moments' and 'Ikigai365 Tune-in' tools.

If you are doing this on the weekend and can invest a bit more time, say between forty-five and sixty minutes, we recommend you find a quiet space and indulge yourself with Ikigai365 myPace Nourishment Tools.

Remember: Ikigai is a blend of both psychology and philosophy. While its roots are in Japan, the concept is universal, human, and evergreen in nature. To borrow a metaphor from automobiles, whether you're in fourth gear today or the first, we have a tool for you. And while there is no 'cruise control' in life, we hope this becomes your trusted GPS that helps you navigate whatever life throws at you.

So, we sincerely wish you myPace as you embark on the next phase of your Ikigai journey. We also hope that Ikigai365 has sown a few more seeds that you will tune-into and take actions as you experience your Ikigai365 journey!

myIkigai365 Toolkit

What Makes Your Heart Smile?

(This exercise takes approximately 10–15 mins to complete.
Recommended frequency is once every week.)

Current Date: **Current Time:**

Think about last week. Pick a memory from your own life last week
that **made your heart smile.**

Where were you?

_____

What time of the day was it?

_____

What were you doing?

_____

Who else was with you? Or were you alone?

_____

Who all did you notice around you?

_____

Which particular moment and setting made your heart smile?

_____

What did it make you feel like?

_____

How did your sense of sight, hearing, kinetics, touch, and smell feel?

_____

Write down the **one thing** that you can try and start today in your
daily life based on some of the elements in the reflection above.

_____

_____

_____

Ikigai365 Reflection Moments: Coffee Date with Yourself

(This exercise takes approximately 10–15 minutes to complete. Recommended frequency is once every week.)

How about a coffee date with the most important person? You. You can start by talking the following steps:

A. **Set a Date**: Try to take out time daily, but if not, aim for once a week. Block it off in your calendar like any other appointment.

B. **Choose Your Space**: Find a spot that feels special to you—whether it's a quiet corner in your home, your office, a garden, or your favourite café. This should be a space where you feel relaxed and comfortable to reflect.

C. **What's Brewing in Your Mind?** During this time, let your thoughts flow freely. Write down anything that comes to mind—whether it's feelings, experiences, or insights. This is your moment to notice and appreciate the things that may otherwise go unnoticed.

This simple practice helps you reconnect with yourself and reflect on your journey.

Coffee Date with Yourself

(This exercise takes approximately 10–15 mins to complete.
Recommended frequency is once every week.)

Date: Time: Place:

FEELINGS

- _____

- _____

EXPERIENCES

- _____

- _____

INSIGHTS

- _____

- _____

OTHER POINTS

- _____

- _____

Next coffee date:

Notes to remember:

DESIGN YOUR BEAUTIFUL DAY

(This exercise takes approximately 20–30 mins to complete.
Recommended frequency is once every month.)

Now, let's do an exercise in the not-too-distant future.

So, let's design 'My beautiful day'.

Keep it as real and as detailed as possible within your current environment, commitments, and constraints, but include as much as you can that will make you experience the 'most beautiful day ever', the one which you never want to end and will savour, because it makes you feel alive every moment.

When you're planning the day, a few things you can consider:

- Involve others
- Savour details
- Break routine
- Expect twists and turns
- Try to incorporate nature
- Try something new

Your Thoughts

_____

_____

_____

_____

_____

_____

_____

Iki-ga-ii-na[1]

Savour the Moment with Six Senses

(This exercise takes approximately 20–30 minutes to complete. Recommended frequency is once every month.)

We will now try to activate all your five senses.

- Five senses of sight/touch/taste/smell/sound.
- Emotional sense that help you feel that the here-and-now is special
- *(Futsu-wo-Tokubetsu-ni-suru)* > Finding the special in the everyday ordinary

---

Take a slow and deep breath. Use any counting technique that you feel helps you 'slow down'.

(E.g. 1-2-3-4-5 Breathe-in > 1-2-3-4-5 Hold > 5-4-3-2-1 Breathe Out

Repeat a few times till you begin to feel a bit relaxed and calm.

---

[1] 'Iki-ga-ii-na' has two meanings in Japanese.

The first is as a phrase expressing a concept similar to 'a reason for living.' Here, 'Ikigai' is the key term, meaning just that—'a reason for being' or 'life's purpose.' In this case, 'na' functions as a sentence-ending particle.

The second meaning is more literal: 'good breathing.' Here, 'iki' means 'breath,' 'ga' and 'na' are grammatical particles, and 'ii' means 'good.'

Three to Four Things You Can See

Focus on your eyes for the next minute or so. Notice a few (three to four) different objects that you see around you with your eyes. Now find one object that is usually present, but you don't usually notice or pay attention to. What is it? Say it aloud.

How does noticing it make you feel?

Two to Three Different Sensations You Can Touch/Feel

Focus on your skin and body for the next minute or so. Notice a few (two to three) different sensations you can touch/feel on any part of your body with your skin. Now find one sensation that is usually present, but you don't usually notice or pay attention to. What is it? Say it aloud.

How does noticing it make you feel?

One to Two Different Tastes in Your Mouth

Focus on your tongue for the next minute or so. Notice a few (one to two) different tastes in your mouth with your tongue. Now find one taste that is usually present, but you don't usually notice or pay attention to. What is it? Say it aloud.

How does noticing it make you feel?

Two to Three Different Smells That You Can Savour

Focus on your nose for the next minute or so. Notice a few (Two to Three) different smells that you can savour in your nose. Now find one smell that is usually present but you don't usually notice or pay attention to. What is it? Say it aloud.

How does noticing it make you feel?

Three to Four Different Sounds That You Can Hear

Focus on your ears for the next minute or so. Notice a few (three to four) different sounds that you can hear in your ear. Now find one sound that is usually present, but you don't usually notice or pay attention to. What is it? Say it aloud.

How does noticing it make you feel?

Take a slow and deep breath again.

Having savoured a few moments, please write down the one thing that you plan to start today in your daily life, based on some of the elements or emotions triggered in the reflection above. How can you transform some ordinary life routines into special moments that make you feel alive?

_____

_____

_____

Letter From Your
Future Self

There is a solution-focused approach within brief therapy.[33] This concept was developed in the 1980s in Milwaukee, US, by a team of family therapy practitioners, led by Steve de Shazer and Insoo Kim Berg, who worked with drinking problems, among others.

Devoted to Milton H. Erickson, de Shazer wrote influenced research papers.

Erik Erikson is best known for his work on the eight stages of psychosocial development and introduction of moratorium into psychology, along with his work on identity.

On the other hand, Milton H. Erickson is known as a hypnotherapist and an influential figure in the practice of family therapy and effective psychotherapy. de Shazer was influenced by Erickson's view of looking at time. The hypnotic phenomenon of 'age regression' involves going back in time to an earlier time and reliving an earlier memory in image. This method is influenced by psychoanalysis in the way that if you have a problem in the present because of a childhood experience, let's go back and re-experience that old memory to fix your current condition.

Erickson was rich in ideas and used hypnotic induction to 'transit the timeline into the future', instead of going back in time.[34] In the hypnotic state, the suggestion was given that 'you will see the future state in your crystal ball', the improved state was seen in the crystal ball, and after waking up from the hypnotic state, the client naturally forgot it, amnesia would occur, and then went about his daily life and later came back to report in the next interview that person had behave as the story in his/her crystal ball.

They were doing what they had said in their crystal ball in their real-life behaviour. We could interpret that the clients may have answers within.

This method is referred to as the 'crystal ball technique' or 'pseudo-orientation in time technique'. de Shazer discusses the similarities between a solution-focused approach and Erickson's Crystal Ball Technique.

One of the solution-focused approach practitioners in the team is Yvonne Dolan. She introduced the 'letter from your future self' exercise, back when she has been invited a workshop in Japan in 2014—and we will focus on it.[35]

Letter From Your Future Self

(This exercise takes at least 60 minutes to complete. Recommended frequency is once every year.)

You are now starting an exercise in which we need you to imagine that you will receive a letter from your future self.

The below set of instructions will guide you to write the letter . . .

- Choose a specific date in the future: one year later, five years later, ten years later, and so on. This is the date on which your future self is writing a letter to you in this exercise.
- Time has now passed; it is now the specific date you have chosen in the future, and you have grown into your future self. Imagine that you are now living ideally: leading a very healthy, fulfilled, and happy life, while coping easily with all your everyday challenges.
- When you are writing this letter, please do not get stuck in whether something is realistically possible or achievable. Without thinking too deeply, just imagine that you have achieved your ideal life.
- Now, think about all the different specific ways in which you overcame various challenges to get here.

- Imagine this future daily life in as specific detail as possible. Where are you living, and how are you spending your time every day? Who are all the people you spend time with every day? How do you feel every day?

Now, please proceed to the next steps and complete the exercise.

Step 1: In the 'Letter from your future self' that you will receive, what is going on in your daily life? Write down and describe it in as much detail as possible.

_____

_____

_____

_____

_____

_____

_____

Step 2: Now, write the letter from your future self. Feel free to handwrite, use colours/pictures/etc, and express yourself freely.

Date:

Dear ....

_____

_____

_____

_____

_____

_____

Read the set of instructions given on the first page of this tool and imagine that you have just received the letter from your future self.

How do you feel? What are you thinking now? Write down and describe your strongest feelings/thoughts below.

_____

_____

_____

_____

_____

_____

_____

Write down your latest feelings and thoughts about what shifts you would like to make in your own life, starting tomorrow.

_____

_____

_____

_____

_____

_____

_____

Doh-Sa Therapy Practice

(This exercise takes at least 60 minutes to complete. Recommended frequency is anytime you feel the need step back/reflect/get a boost.)

Self-care using the Clinical Dohsa Therapy
By Prof. Akihiro Hasegawa

In 1964, a report was brought to Gosaku Naruse, a professor at Kyushu University. It stated that when a child with cerebral palsy was induced into a hypnotic state, their body, which was otherwise difficult to move, could perform movements during hypnosis, and when out of that state, the paralysis returned.[36] *Dohsa* in Japanese is called 'moving the body'.

Dohsa is a series of processes from the generation in a person's mind of an intention or image of planning to move the body, to the striving of applying the appropriate force to the appropriate part of the body to achieve the intended physical movement, which can be observed as 'body movement'.[37]

Dohsa therapy is called when psychological support is required mainly.

When Prof. Hasegawa devised the elements of Ikigai model, he incorporated the sense of self control used in the clinical *Dohsa-hou* into the feeling of Ikigai. Sense of self control refers to the feeling that agent moves own body independently by oneself, and that the mind is activated and actively working on it. The Clinical Dohsa-hou works with the mind through the body. In this tool, we will show you how to use the Clinical Dohsa-hou as self-care.[38]

Doh-Sa Therapy Practice

Doh-a task: Shoulder raising task on a chair

(This exercise takes at least 60 minutes to complete. Recommended frequency is anytime you feel the need to step back/reflect/get a boost.)

01

SIT UP

Sit up on the floor in a chair or cross-legged position.

02

RATE HOW YOU FEEL

Rate how you are feeling at the moment on a 10-point scare. 'If the highest score is 10 and the lowest score is 1, what is your current feeling? And rate your feeling.

03

CONDUCT BODY SCAN

After assessing current feelings, a body scan is conducted. From the top of the head, slowly and over time, check how tense the body is, moving the body slightly until you reach the bottom of the feet. When you reach the bottom of the feet, now check the areas of tension towards the top of the head.

04

SIT STRAIGHT

Sit with your back away from the backrest and your back straight. Also sit with both feet firmly on the floor so that the knees and heels are about shoulder-width apart. Move the upper body back and forth, left and right, to find an even point so that the buttocks are sitting evenly.

CROSSED-LEGGED POSITION

Sit with a straight back. Bring both knees as close to the floor as possible. Move your upper body back and forth and side to side to find an even place so that your buttocks are sitting evenly.

CHOOSE AND RAISE SHOULDER

Determine which shoulder to raise. Slowly raise that shoulder straight up.

CONTINUE RAISING SHOULDER

Try to raise the shoulder and see if you feel any difficulty in raising it in the middle. If it becomes difficult to raise, stop raising and wait for a moment. Maintain the shoulder at that height. Tense and relax part of the body, not the whole body, to control itself.

PAY ATTENTION TO THE SHOULDER

While the shoulders remain at that height, turn your attention to the area around the shoulders. If there is tension, relax the tension that is present, while maintaining shoulder height. If you wait while maintaining shoulder height, you may relax. Pay attention to whether there is any tension from the shoulders to the neck. If you wait while maintaining shoulder height and try to relax the area you have focused on, you may find that the area relaxes and the shoulder feels more comfortable.

RAISE SHOULDER AGAIN

When a feeling of relaxation is felt around the shoulder and neck area, raise the shoulder straight up again. Even if you are not sure if the force has relaxed, try to raise the shoulders straight up again.

REPEAT STEPS 6–9

Repeat Steps 6–9 several times.

LOWER SHOULDER

When you feel that the shoulder cannot go up any further, stop lifting. Wait a little and try to raise it again. If the shoulder can be raised, raise it. If the shoulder cannot be raised, slowly start to lower it. Ask yourself to pay attention to the change in you while controlling yourself.

REPEAT STEPS 6–11

Repeat two or three times with one set of Steps 6–11.

DO IT FOR THE OPPOSITE SHOULDER

Repeat Steps 7–13 for the opposite shoulder.

ASK QUESTIONS

Check with yourself as needed. 'How did you feel when you lifted your shoulder?', 'How did you feel on the way down?' Ask yourself to understand the experience of working on it.

15

MEASURE EFFECTIVENESS

Ask effectiveness measurement questions from time to time to determine whether the implementation is appropriate or whether it is ineffective and should be discontinued.

Key points

1. Raise your shoulders while enjoying the feeling that you are moving your 'body'.
2. The aim is not to raise the shoulders as much as possible, but to raise them as a result.
3. The upper body may tilt in the opposite direction to the shoulder being raised, so correct the posture by 'returning the posture so that the shoulder rides on the hip of the side being raised' during the exercise. Similarly, be attentive to whether the neck is tilted or unnecessary movement or force is applied to the elbows and wrists. Try to maintain proper posture.
4. At a good break in the implementation, conduct scaling questions about 'how you feel now' to monitor changes and measure effectiveness from time to time. When a certain level of effectiveness has been achieved, move the task to the opposite shoulder. If the scaling values do not drop after five minutes or more of work on the first shoulder, the exercise may be terminated because you may feel tired later on and a different approach may be appropriate.
5. If pain or discomfort is felt in a body part other than the shoulder, slowly move and relax the complained-about area other than the shoulder. When the pain that caused the complaint is reduced, return to the shoulder area and work on it again.

Connecting The Dots

(This exercise takes at least 60 minutes to complete.
Recommended frequency is once every year.)

The Connecting the Dots tool helps you reflect in the present, so that you can leverage and learn from your past to strengthen your future identity and self-worth.

Identity is formed by reflecting on questions like 'Who am I?' and 'Where am I going?'

It involves integrating various self-images developed since childhood into a cohesive sense of self during adolescence. This sense of identity is shaped by both personal experiences and interactions with society, which influence how we see ourselves and how we believe others perceive us.[39]

During adolescence, young people often reassess their values and develop a stronger sense of purpose or 'Ikigai' as they navigate new environments, like moving on to higher education.[40] This period marks a turning point where individuals reflect on their past, present, and future, shaping their identity and sense of meaning in life.

The Connecting the Dots tool supports this process by encouraging reflection on one's experiences and values, helping to strengthen both identity and purpose, much like the concept of Ikigai.

Connecting The Dots

(This exercise takes at least 60 mins to complete.
Recommended frequency is once every year.)

Have you ever thought about these questions:

- Who am I?
- Why do I think what I think?
- Why do I act the way I do?
- What is the impact I want to make in this world?
- What should be the roadmap to defining my purpose?

In a mind map format, please note down your:
Love/Skills: ....
Thoughts and beliefs: ....
Actions: ....
Impact you wish to make: ....

PAST	PRESENT	PRESENT
Love/skills thoughts and beliefs	Your actions	What impact you would like to make
-------------------------	-------------------------	-------------------------
-------------------------	-------------------------	-------------------------
-------------------------	-------------------------	-------------------------
-------------------------	-------------------------	-------------------------

Lifeline Map

(This exercise takes at least 60 minutes to complete.
Recommended frequency is once every year.)

This tool encourages reflection and projection by creating a visual representation of your personal past, present, and future. The process helps you reflect on the twists and turns along the path of your life, as well as imagine future possibilities and inevitable challenges.[41]

The vertical axis is used to mark highs (like, feeling happy or good) and lows (like, feeling bad or low).

The horizontal axis is anchored in the present (today) and moves in two directions with specific steps to help you identify your sources of Ikigai throughout your journey.

The steps into the past start from the near past (last week, last month) and expand further (last year, last few years, last decade), continuing in decade-steps all the way to your birth.

The steps into the future similarly begin with near-future timeframes (next week, next month) and expand further (next year, next decade), projecting two–three decades ahead.

These steps are designed to help you recall or imagine important episodes and the flow of key life events—such as childhood, school entry and graduation, higher education, employment and career progression, personal friendships and relationships, marriage, children, etc—all within the timeline of your life.

Once you have marked the various episodes and noted the corresponding highs and lows for each, connect the episodes with lines to form lifelines. This visual helps with self-reflection, showing where your lifeline has formed peaks and valleys over time.

IKIGAI365 Lifeline Mapping

(This exercise takes at least 60 mins to complete.
Recommended frequency is once every year)

	My Past			My Present	My Future		
	Birth, teens and early years	Last decade	Last year	Last week/ month	Today (here and now)	Next week/ month	Next year	Next decade and beyond
Feeling high								
++								
+								
Neutral								
-								
–								
Feeling low								
	Birth, teens and early years	Last decade	Last year	Last week/ month	Today (here and now)	Next week/ month	Next year	Next decade and beyond
	My Past				My Present	My Future		

Ikigai > Hatarakigai

(This exercise takes approximately 20–30 minutes to complete. Recommended frequency is anytime you feel the need step back/ reflect/get a boost.)

This tool is designed to broaden your view of the different roles you play in daily life and to help you understand that Ikigai (a life worth living) is much broader than hatarakigai (work worth doing).

While both concepts are rooted in the search for value, purpose, and meaning in our personal and professional spheres, Ikigai is a universal human superset that applies to all people at all stages of life. Hatarakigai, on the other hand, applies only to those engaged in professional activities that earn a livelihood.

Ikigai is relevant every day for every human—from birth to death—while hatarakigai is generally relevant only for those in the workforce, and typically only until retirement.[42]

This distinction makes Ikigai journeys beneficial not only for people in the professional workforce, but also for students, homemakers, and retirees.

This tool will also help you reflect on and reprioritize the roles, people, places, and activities that matter to you intrinsically— those that trigger positive or negative emotions in your daily life. It helps you differentiate between:

a) Sources of Ikigai
b) Familial duties and social commitments
c) Sources of livelihood

Enjoy the self-discovery exercise below, designed to help you identify your own sources of Ikigai. To help you get started, consider the following questions:

a) How much money is enough? Just enough for your needs, or enough for both needs and some wants? Have you ever felt that if what you had yesterday was not enough, then most probably what you will have tomorrow will also not be enough?

b) What is the primary difference between your own sources of Ikigai and hatarakigai? What are your sources of Ikigai that give you a sense of feeling alive? What kind of work makes you feel fulfilled—so much so that you would do it without getting paid or expecting any recognition?

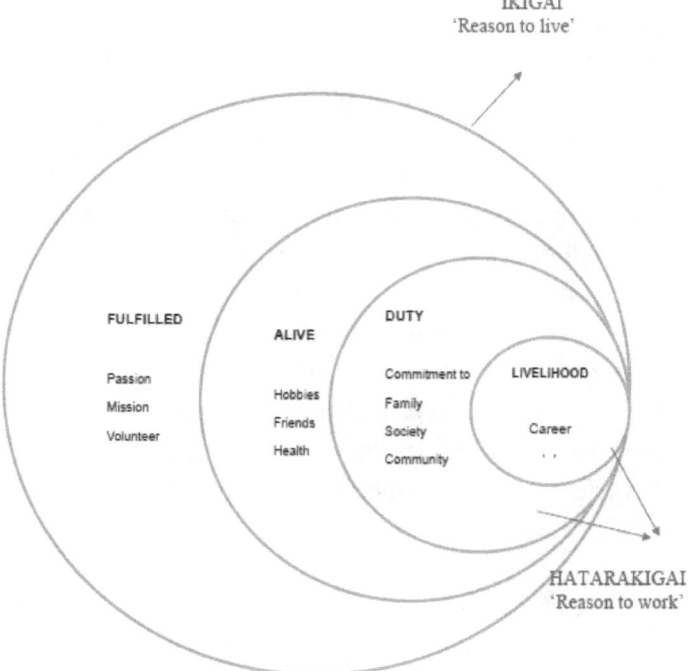

Fill Your Cup

With more and more Ikigai sources

(This exercise takes at least 60 minutes to complete. Recommended frequency is anytime you feel the need to step back/reflect/get a boost.)

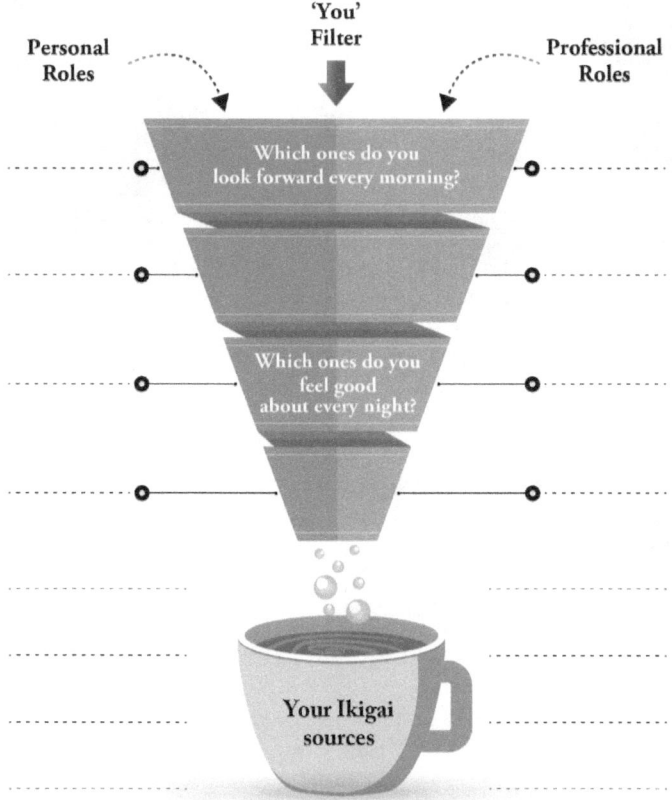

Ikigai365 Reflections > Action Tool

(This exercise takes approximately 60 minutes or longer to complete)
(Recommended frequency: Anytime you feel the need to step back/reflect/get a boost)

Here and Now
Present feelings or emotions
you are experiencing

Past memories
or experiences
triggered

Future
hopes or dreams
rekindled

What change
do you
choose to make

Now, what is the one action you will take today or start tomorrow ?

I will

This is neither 'the end' nor 'the beginning'.
Just a stepping stone in your own Ikigai journey.
This is Ikigai365.
Your journey to feeling alive and fulfilled every day!
Across all the different seasons of life.

Endnotes

1   Kamiya, M., 1966. *Ikigai ni tsuite* (About Ikigai). Tokyo: Misuzu Shobo, Ltd. (in Japanese).
2   Hasegawa, A., Fujiwara, Y, and Hoshi, T., 2001. The review of IKIGAI on the relationship of Ikigai and well-being in the elderly. *Comprehensive Urban Studies*, (75), pp.147–170. (In Japanese).
3   Hasegawa, A., 2003. Empirical study of the "IKIGAI (purpose in life/reason(s) for living)" for the elderly according to the area. Doctoral thesis, Tokyo Metropolitan University, Graduate School, Division of Urban Science. Ph.D. in Urban Science. (In Japanese).
4   Hasegawa, A., Fujiwara, Y, and Hoshi, T., 2003. The structure of "IKIGAI" - Analysis of the covariance structure of the "object of IKIGAI" and "feelings accompanying (the object of IKIGAI)". *Journal of the Japanese Society of Care Managers*, 2, pp.65–79. (In Japanese).
5   Deci, E., 1971. Effects of externally mediated rewards on intrinsic motivation. *Journal of Personality and Social Psychology*, 18(1), pp.105–115.
6   Deci, E.L. & Ryan, R.M., 1985. Intrinsic motivation and self-determination in human behavior. New York: Plenum.
7   Maslow, A. H., 1943. A theory of human motivation. *Psychological Review*, 50(4), pp.370–396.

8   Williams, K. K. and Jarvis, B., 2006. Cyberball: A program for use in research on interpersonal ostracism and acceptance. *Behaviour Research Methods*, 38(1), pp.174–180.

9   The Asahi Shimbun, 2024. Survey: Almost 14% of all homes in Japan found to be vacant. *The Asahi Shimbun*. Available at: https://www.asahi.com/ajw/articles/15252431.

10   Nippon, 2024. Number of vacant homes in Japan reaches record 9 million. *Nippon*. Available at: https://www.nippon.com/en/japan-data/h01987/.

11   Rogers, C. R., 1959. A theory of therapy, personality, and interpersonal relationships, as developed in the client-centered framework. In: S. Koch, ed., *Psychology: A study of a science*, Vol. 3. Formulations of the person and the social context. New York: McGraw-Hill, pp.184–256.

12   Ryan, R. M. and Deci, E. L., 2000. Self-determination theory and the facilitation of intrinsic motivation, social development, and well-being. *American Psychologist*, 55(1), pp.68–78.

13   The Asahi Shimbun, 2024. 1 in 6 elderly in Japan estimated to have dementia in 2060. *The Asahi Shimbun*. Available at: https://www.asahi.com/ajw/articles/15259335.

14   National Library of Medicine, 2023. Physical activity and exercise for the prevention and management of mild cognitive impairment and dementia: a collaborative international guideline. *National Library of Medicine*. Available at: https://pmc.ncbi.nlm.nih.gov/articles/PMC10587099/.

15   Erickson, M. H., Rossi, E. L., and Rossi, S. I., 1976. *Hypnotic realities: The induction of clinical hypnosis and forms of indirect suggestion*. Irvington Publishers.

16   Baumeister, R. & Leary, M., 1995. The need to belong: Desire for interpersonal attachments as a fundamental human motivation. *Psychological Bulletin*, 117(3), pp. 497-529.

17   Connolly Cove, 2024. The Samurai Code: Unveiling Bushido's influence on Japanese warrior ethos. *Connolly Cove*.

Available at: https://www.connollycove.com/the-samurai-code-exploring-bushido/.

18 Hayes, S. C., Strosahl, K. D., and Wilson, K. G., 2012. *Acceptance and commitment therapy: The process and practice of mindful change* (2nd ed). New York: Guilford Press.

19 Gouldner, A. W., 1960. The norm of reciprocity: A preliminary statement. *American Sociological Review*, 25(2), pp.161–178.

20 Taylor, S.E., 1983. Adjustment to threatening events: A theory of cognitive adaptation. *American Psychologist*, 38(11), pp.1161-1173.

21 Kashdan, T. B. and Steger, M. F., 2007. Curiosity and pathways to well-being and meaning in life: Traits, states, and everyday behaviours. *Motivation and Emotion*, 31(3), pp.159–173.

22 Kashdan, T.B. et al., 2018. The five-dimensional curiosity scale: Capturing the bandwidth of curiosity and identifying four unique subgroups of curious people. *Journal of Research in Personality*, 73, pp.130–149.

23 Csikszentmihalyi, M., 1990. *Flow: The Psychology of Optimal Experience*. New York: Harper and Row.

24 Norton, M., 2024. *The Ritual Effect: From Habit to Ritual, Harness the Surprising Power of Everyday Actions*. Scribner.

25 Brain Training Game improves executive functions and processing speed in the elderly: A randomized controlled trial, 2012. *Plos One*. Available at: https://journals.plos.org/plosone/article?id=10.1371/journal.pone.0048669.

26 Grabbe, J. W., 2011. Sudoku and working memory performance for older adults. *ResearchGate*. Available at: https://www.researchgate.net/publication/260372702_Sudoku_and_working_memory_performance_for_older_adults.

27 Ulrich, R. S., Simons, R. F., Losito, B. D., Fiorio, E., Miles, M. A., and Zelson, M., 1991. Stress recovery during exposure to natural and urban environments. *Journal of Environmental Psychology*, 11, pp.201–230.

28 Bratman, G. N., Hamilton, J. P., Hahn, K. S., Daily, G. C., and Gross, J. J., 2015. Nature experience reduces rumination and subgenual prefrontal cortex activation. *Proceedings of the National Academy of Sciences (PNAS)*, 112(28), pp.8567–72.

29 Shiota, M. N., Keltner, D., and Mossman, A., 2007. The nature of awe: Elicitors, appraisals, and effects on self-concept. Cognition and Emotion, 21(5), pp.944–963.

30 Simonton, D.K., 1999. Creativity from a historiometric perspective. In: R.J. Sternberg, ed. *Handbook of creativity*. Cambridge: Cambridge University Press, pp.116–133.

31 Cornelius, R.R., 1996. *The science of emotion: Research and tradition in the psychology of emotions*. Upper Saddle River, NJ: Prentice-Hall.

32 Hasegawa, A. (2023) 'The current state and future directions of research on 'Ikigai' at 2023', *Toyo Eiwa University Psychological Counseling Centre Bulletin*, 27, pp. 32-29. (in Japanese)

33 de Shazer, S. & Berg, I.K., 1991. The brief therapy tradition. In: J.H. Weakland & W.A. Ray, eds. Propagations: Thirty years of influence from the Mental Research Institute. New York: Haworth, pp. 249–252.

34 Erickson, M.H., 1954. Pseudo-orientation in time as a hypnotherapeutic procedure. *Journal of Clinical and Experimental Hypnosis*, 2, pp.261–283.

35 Okamoto, K., Kobayashi, Y. & Hasegawa, A. (eds.), 2023. *Brief psychotherapy for self-care: Meditation techniques, NLP, clinical Dohsa-hou, biofeedback*. Kanagawa: Shunpusha. (in Japanese)
Dolan, Y., 2014. Handouts at the Brief Therapy Network Japan 18th Conference, 15–16 February 2014, Tokyo, Japan.

36 Kobayashi, S., 1966. Rehabilitation of cerebral palsy. In: G. Naruse, ed. *Educational hypnotism*. Tokyo: Seishinshobo, pp.279–290. (in Japanese)

37 Naruse, G., 1995. *Basic clinical movement science.* Tokyo: Gakuensha. (in Japanese)
38 Okamoto, K., Kobayashi, Y. & Hasegawa, A. (eds.), 2023. *Brief psychotherapy for self-care: Meditation techniques, NLP, clinical Dohsa-hou, biofeedback.* Kanagawa: Shunpusha. (in Japanese)
39 Erikson, E.H., 1959. Identity and the life cycle. New York: International Universities Press.
    Erikson, E.H., 1968. Identity: youth and crisis. New York: W.W. Norton.
40 Matsui, M. *2024 Examining the relationship between "ikigai" and identity in the early 20s: Master's thesis in 2023, Department of Human Sciences, Graduate School of Human Sciences, Toyo Eiwa University.* (in JAPANESE)
41 Satoh, N., 2024. *A study of posttraumatic growth (PTG) among disaster relief workers - focusing on government employees who experienced the complex disaster of the Great East Japan Earthquake.* Master's thesis, Department of Human Sciences, Graduate School of Human Sciences, Toyo Eiwa University. (in Japanese).
42 Kobayashi, S., 2021. *An examination of the awareness of welfare service workers for people with intellectual disabilities towards "ikigai" of their users and the psychological processes involved in providing support.* Master's thesis, Department of Human Sciences, Graduate School of Human Sciences, Toyo Eiwa University. (in Japanese).
    Kaminaga, M., 2024. *A research on the "ikigai" and "hataraki-gai" in late adulthood and early middle age.* Master's thesis, Department of Human Sciences, Graduate School of Human Sciences, Toyo Eiwa University. (in Japanese).